Thë ·Läst Öënërätiön

Jšläm
in
Biblë Präphëcy

Dr. Paul Felter

The Last Generation
Islam in Bible Prophecy
Version 3.0 (2015)
Version 4.0 (2023)

Published by
Harpazo Publishing Company
Houston, Texas
www.breadoflife.media

ISBN: 978-0-9829954-0-2

Printed in the United States of America

All Scripture quotes are from the public domain King James
Version.

Paul Felter; Master of Arts in Biblical Studies, PhD in Christian
Apologetics

This book is dedicated to the Lord Jesus Christ. Without the leading and revelation of the Holy Spirit in preparing this work, it would not have been possible.

Table of Contents

Preface

I wrote the original version of this book in 2010 with an update in 2015. But now in 2023-24 I felt the Lord leading me to do another update. With the war in Israel and the rise in antisemitism, we must understand the source and consequences of this worldwide phenomenon. Hamas and the so-called Palestinian refugees garner more support worldwide than the victim of their attack, Israel.

Every day the United Nations decries Israel's effort to eradicate Hamas calling for peace and security. Could this be the stage for the 7-year covenant of Daniel 9:27?

Within the pages of this book, you will gain a Biblical understanding of the end times and the role of Islam in Bible prophecy. While most prophecy experts are looking for a revived Roman empire or a rebuilding of ancient Babylon, the true Biblical scenario is playing out right before our eyes. Islam is the idolatrous whore that rides the beast and Mecca is that great city that reigns over many nations.

The world stage is set for the breaking of the seven seals, the blowing of the seven trumpets, and the pouring of the seven bowls of the wrath of God.

If all the last days events are at hand, how much closer is the rapture of the church, the body of Christ? What a glorious day to be alive!

"Looking for that blessed hope, and the glorious appearing of the great God and our Saviour Jesus Christ;" - Titus 2:13 KJV

Introduction

This book was created in response to the need for a comprehensive systematic guide through the Prophetic scriptures. Much of what is available today is fragmented and singularly topical. I have incorporated all the major Prophetic topics and Scripture verses in this guide with the purpose of giving the student a complete study on the Second Coming of Jesus Christ and the accompanying events.

During this study we will cover Prophetic Scriptures from Genesis chapter ten through the Book of Revelation. The Book of Revelation is the last book in the Bible for a good reason. You must have a clear understanding of the previous 65 books to properly understand the Book of Revelation. Most of the New Testament prophetic Scriptures are an affirmation of the Old Testament prophetic passages, with the notable exception of the rapture of the church, the Body of Christ, so our study will take us through much of the Old Testament.

Before we get started, I want to refresh your mind with a few high-level concepts that will enhance your understanding. First, please decide now that you will set aside any preconceived notions of Bible Prophecy and open your heart and mind to what is clearly written in the Scriptures. There are many Church traditions and teachings of men that are simply not found in the Bible. As we move through our study, I will point out differences between the classical western view of a topic and the Biblical texts. You will be absolutely amazed at what the Bible actually says.

Secondly, the most important rule of Biblical interpretation is "stay in context." In our study I will stress this rule and you will quickly notice that the Bible explains itself. The Bible is its own commentary. I cannot stress enough the concept of "stay in context" for it is routinely broken by many Prophecy teachers and leads to much error and confusion in the Body of Christ. The Apostle Peter clearly states in 2 Peter 1:20 *"Knowing this first, that no prophecy of the scripture is of any private interpretation.*" This is a clear command against taking a verse here and there and making a doctrine. Many are guilty of cherry-picking verses that support their presuppositions yet totally ignoring other passages that refute their assumptions. We must stay in the context of the surrounding verses, the chapter, the book and the entire Bible. Most are familiar with this concept, but few practice it.

Thirdly, understand that the 66 books of the Bible are one contiguous message given to us by the Holy Spirit and the entire work speaks of the Lord Jesus Christ. When Jesus met the two disciples on the road to Emmaus Luke recounts "*And beginning at Moses and all the prophets, he expounded unto them in all the Scriptures the things concerning himself.*" Jesus also states in the Gospel of John, "*Search the Scriptures; for in them ye think ye have eternal life: and they are they which testify of me.*"

Fourthly, throughout the entire Bible there are only two seeds. Everyone is either the seed of the Lord or the seed of the devil. This division is first stated in Genesis chapter three where the Lord places a curse on the serpent; "*And I will put enmity between thee and the woman, and between thy seed and her seed; it shall bruise thy head, and thou shalt bruise his heel.*"

We see the two seeds in Isaac and Ishmael, Jacob and Esau, Joseph and his brothers, Elijah and Jezebel, baby Jesus and Herod, Jesus and Judas, Jesus(second coming) and the Antichrist, and many others. The two seeds are clearly revealed in the parable of the wheat and tares in Matthew chapter 13 and again in chapter 25 with the separation of the sheep and goats. Please keep in mind the concept of the two seeds in our study as it will help clarify prophetic details.

As we exegete the scriptures pertaining to end times prophecy, we will compare the traditional revived Roman Empire/European Union/European Antichrist paradigm with the alternative paradigm of a Middle Eastern Empire and an Islamic Antichrist.

Lastly, the Apostle Paul instructs us to "*Study to show thyself approved unto God, a workman that needeth not to be ashamed, rightly dividing the word of truth*" (2 Tim 2:15). We are to rightly divide the Word of truth. For example, Israel is Israel, the Church is the Church; each is a distinct entity. Those that teach that the Church has replaced Israel display a profound confusion about Bible Prophecy. There are a great many prophecies directly related to Israel All the prophesies in the Old Testament are for Israel. Attempting to apply them to the Church is lunacy.

Prophetic scriptures are found in many books of the Bible. These are like pieces of a puzzle; one must study them all to piece together a picture of the events surrounding the Second Coming of Christ, the Day of the Lord. Since we see through a glass darkly, it's not easy to piece it all together, but we should at least be aware of each prophecy so that we understand what is coming upon the earth. Knowledge dissuades fear.

Also, Bible prophecy is not prediction and fulfillment as we have been taught. Some end time Bible prophecies are patterns repeated several times throughout history with their final fulfillment happening during the 7-year Tribulation. An example of this is the Abomination of Desolation perpetrated by Antiochus Euphonies, the Seleucid King, around 170 to 160 B.C. Caesar Pompeii repeated this around 39 B.C. Later the Romans erected a statue of Jupiter on the Temple Mount. Today we have another abomination of desolation sitting on the Temple Mount, the Dome of the Rock Mosque. Prophecy is pattern; what has gone around comes around.

There are over 30 distinct prophecies concerning the first coming of Jesus as the Messiah, the Son of Joseph. Each of these prophecies was literally fulfilled. There are over eight times as many prophecies concerning the Second Coming of Jesus Christ. The world stage is now set for their fulfillment. There is no reason not to expect a literal fulfillment of those also.

The prophet Isaiah writes:

"Remember the former things of old: for I am God, and there is none else; I am God, and there is none like me, **Declaring the end from the beginning**, *and from ancient times the things that are not yet done, saying,* **My counsel shall stand, and I will do all my pleasure**: *Calling a ravenous bird from the east, the man that executeth my counsel from a far country:* **yea, I have spoken it, I will also bring it to pass; I have purposed it, I will also do it.**" *— Isaiah 46:9-11*

In this study you will immediately notice many direct quotes from Scripture. These quotes will have phrases bolded for emphasis. In many places I do not comment on all the bolded phrases so do not skip over them even if you are familiar with the text. Read each word and let the Holy Spirit speak to your heart, after all, He inspired the word.

Thank you for joining me in this tremendous adventure in Biblical Prophecy. We will begin with the Prophet Daniel. Daniel's prophecies are foundational to a correct understanding of the end times so let's get started.

Be sure to read the last chapter on Islam as it is arguably the most important chapter in the book. You must understand Islam to recognize the serious threat it poses to America, our form of government and our way of life.

A word to our Muslim friends:

All the nations named in the Old Testament as receiving the end times wrath and judgment from the Lord are Middle Eastern nations. During this study I will frequently mention characteristics of Islam and some Muslim leaders. However, we love the Muslim people and desire that all come to the saving knowledge of the Lord Jesus Christ. Many are, in fact, leaving Islam and turning to Jesus Christ as Lord and Savior. I believe that the largest end time harvest will come from China and the

Muslim nations. We pray for the Muslim people. Just as we love Germans but despise Nazi-Fascism, love Russians and the Chinese but despise Communism, we love Muslims and pray that the darkness of Islam will be overcome by the light of the glorious Gospel of Jesus Christ.

Pärt Önë

Thë Bëäst Kïngdöms

Chäptër Önë

Nëbuchädnëzzär's Drëäm

The Great Image - Daniel Chapter 2

The Prophecies of the Book of Daniel are foundational to a correct understanding of God's plan for the end times. We begin our study in Daniel chapter two discovering the kingdoms that define the times of the Gentiles. These kingdoms begin with Babylon and end with the kingdom of the Lord Jesus Christ, the Millennial Kingdom.

The Prophet Daniel was an extremely talented young Hebrew taken captive to Babylon in ~604 B.C. to serve in the king's court. King Nebuchadnezzar had a troubling dream but when he awoke the dream had left him. He charges all the wise men to tell him the dream and the interpretation or suffer the penalty of death.

*"The king answered and said to the Chaldeans, The thing is gone from me: if ye will not make known unto me the dream, with the interpretation thereof, **ye shall be cut in pieces, and your houses shall be made a dunghill.**" — Daniel 2:5*

*"Then was the **secret revealed unto Daniel in a night vision**. Then Daniel blessed the God of heaven." — Daniel 2:19*

*"The king answered and said to Daniel, whose name was Belteshazzar, Art thou **able to make known unto me the dream which I have seen, and the interpretation thereof**?" — Daniel 2:26*

*"But there is a God in heaven that revealeth secrets, and maketh known to the king Nebuchadnezzar **what shall be in the latter days**. Thy dream, and the visions of thy head upon thy bed, are these;" — Daniel 2:28*

The Lord gives Daniel the dream and the interpretation in a night vision. This is an example of dual fulfillment. The interpretation was partially fulfilled by subsequent empires following Babylon. The final fulfillment of this dream will be in the "latter days," the 7-year Tribulation.

*"Thou, O king, sawest, and behold a **great image**. This great image, whose brightness was excellent, stood before thee; and the form thereof was terrible. This image's **head was of fine gold, his breast and his arms of silver, his belly and his thighs of brass, His legs of iron, his feet part of iron and part of clay**. Thou sawest till that a **stone** was cut out without hands, which **smote the image upon his feet** that were of iron and clay, and brake them to pieces. **Then was the iron, the clay, the brass, the silver, and the gold, broken to pieces together**, and became like the chaff of the summer threshing floors; and the wind carried them away, that no place was found for them: and the **stone that smote the image became a great mountain, and filled the whole earth**." — Daniel 2:31-35*

King Nebuchadnezzar dreams of a great image with a head of gold, chest and arms of silver, belly and thighs of

2

brass, legs of iron and feet of iron mixed with clay. These four metals represent Gentile kingdoms and have both a near term and a last day's prophetic fulfillment. We need not wonder about the interpretation for the Lord gave the meaning to Daniel in the following verses.

1. *Head of Gold (Babylon)* - *"Thou, O king, art a king of kings: for the God of heaven hath given thee a kingdom, power, and strength, and glory. And wheresoever the children of men dwell, the beasts of the field and the fowls of the heaven hath he given into thine hand, and hath made thee ruler over them all.* **Thou art this head of gold**" — Daniel 2:36-37

2. *Chest and Arms of Silver (Media-Persia)* - *"And after thee shall arise another kingdom inferior to thee"* — Daniel 2:39

3. *Belly and Thighs of Brass (Greece)* - *"and another **third kingdom of brass**, which shall bear rule over all the earth."* — Daniel 2:39

4. *Legs of Iron (Rome???)* - *"And the **fourth kingdom shall be strong as iron**: forasmuch as iron breaketh in pieces and **subdueth all things**: and as iron that **breaketh all these**, shall it break in pieces and bruise."* — Daniel 2:40

Nebuchadnezzar's Babylon is the head of gold. Verse 39 states that "***after thee shall arise another kingdom***"; that kingdom was Media-Persia. Then "another third kingdom" follows, that being the Greek Empire.

The classical interpretation of the legs of iron is the Roman Empire. The feet of iron and clay are thought to be an end time revived Roman Empire considered by many to be the

European Union. Many scholars believe that Rome is the fourth kingdom. However, is Ancient Rome a good fit for the legs of iron and a revived Roman Empire for the feet of iron and clay? Remember, this vision is centered upon Babylon, not Israel, or Europe.

The dream was given to Nebuchadnezzar, not a prophet of Israel. Each succeeding kingdom must conquer the geographical region of Babylon. We see this clearly with the Persian and Grecian empires. They both conquered the entire land area of ancient Babylon and the previous kingdom, but did Rome ever conquer the entirety of Babylon, Persia, and the Grecian Empire?

There is a key phrase in verse 40 that is easily overlooked in the KJV *"as iron breaketh all these, shall it break in pieces and bruise.*" Breaketh all these means that the fourth kingdom will break or conquer "all these" previous kingdoms: Babylon, Media-Persia, and Greece. It is clear that the fourth kingdom must conquer the land area of the previous three.

The eastern boundary of the Roman Empire was the Euphrates River. In 115 A.D. the Roman Army under the rule of Trajan conquered the Parthians in the regions of modern-day Iraq and Iran but Hadrian, the military governor of Syria, re-established the permanent eastern boundary of the Roman Empire at the Euphrates River. Rome never conquered the territory east to the Indus River (border of India) as the Greeks did under Alexander the Great. Therefore, Rome is not the legs of iron, the fourth kingdom, as the region of Babylon and eastward were never a permanent part of the Roman Empire.

*"And the **fourth kingdom shall be strong as iron**: forasmuch as iron breaketh in pieces and subdueth all things: and as iron that breaketh all these, shall it break in pieces and bruise. And whereas thou sawest the feet and toes, part of potters' clay, and part of iron, the **kingdom shall be divided**; but there shall be in it of the strength of the iron, forasmuch as thou sawest the iron mixed with miry clay. And as the toes of the feet were part of iron, and part of clay, so the kingdom shall*

be *partly strong, and partly broken*. *And whereas thou sawest iron mixed with miry clay, they shall mingle themselves with the seed of men: but they shall not cleave one to another, even as iron is not mixed with clay." — Daniel 2:40-43*

When the Roman army conquered a region, they sought to preserve the infrastructure and resources in order to tax commerce. Only those that rebelled against Rome were crushed. In fact, much of the local rule was left to the local leaders of the region. The leaders of Israel during Roman occupation had much authority but could not put someone to death. That is why they had to take Jesus before Pilate, only the Roman governor could authorize a death sentence. Also, much of the Greek influence remained and the Roman influence was simply added hence the term Greco-Roman. The two kingdoms had much in common.

Question: What Empire followed Greece to overtake and break in pieces the Babylonian, Persian and Greek Empires? Remember, the eastern boundary of the Roman Empire was the Euphrates River. I want to say this again, Rome never permanently conquered the region of ancient Babylon and Persia.

What Empire conquered Mesopotamia? **The Islamic Empire!** The Islamic Empire conquered all the land area of Babylon. For that matter, they conquered all of Persia and Greece empires also. The Islamic/Ottoman Empire with its Sultanates and Caliphates are the legs of iron that crushed all previous kingdoms. Islam not only conquers opposing armies but also seeks to destroy the cultures of its victims by converting churches to mosques, replacing governments with theocratic sharia law, and destroying cultural artifacts.

The final form of this forth kingdom will be of iron **mixed** with clay. According to Strongs H6151 "mixed" means *arab (arav)* or Arabian. Where is the religious center of Islam? Mecca, Arabia.

A mixed and mingled people of Arabia (Middle East) will be part of the final fourth kingdom. We will examine this mixed and mingled people later in the book. Islam is the legs of iron and the last days revived Islamic Caliphate will be the feet of iron and clay. The 10 toes of iron and clay correspond to the 10 kings of the last empire as we shall also see later.

Who meets the criteria for the fourth empire, Rome, or Islam? When Islam conquers a region, they institute Sharia law and seek to destroy the previous cultures. Just look at the nations of the Middle East. The fourth kingdom of iron is the Islamic/Ottoman Empire. The feet of iron and clay are the revived Islamic Caliphate soon to appear in the Middle East.

ISIS destroying Assyrian artifacts in Nimrud, The Independent, UK

The Muslim Brotherhood was in the news in 2011 with all the unrest in Egypt and several other Middle Eastern nations. This group was formed in 1928 after the fall of the Ottoman Empire and the disbanding of the Caliphate with the sole purpose of reuniting the Caliphate. The current political climate in the Middle East is ripe for the formation of the Caliphate giving some sense of political stability and power to Islamic nations. Turkey is now preparing for this role as peacemaker in the Middle East.

As of this update, Hamas is in the news daily, along with Hezbollah, and Iran. Hamas' barbarism and butchery are unprecedented in modern times. The Muslim Brotherhood started Hamas in 1987. Hamas claims to be the revived Caliphate and were garnering much support both political and financial before their attack on Israel. Only time will tell whether Hamas, or some other Muslim group or state will rise to lead the 10 kings spoken of many times in prophetic scriptures. Hamas is not radical Islam, it is Islam!

*"And **in the days of these kings shall the God of heaven set up a kingdom, which shall never be destroyed**: and the kingdom shall not be left to other people, but it shall break in pieces and consume all these kingdoms, and **it shall stand for ever**. Forasmuch as thou sawest that the **stone was cut out of the mountain without hands, and that it brake in pieces the iron, the brass, the clay, the silver, and the gold**; the great God hath made known to the king what shall come to pass hereafter: and the dream is certain, and the interpretation thereof sure."* — Daniel 2:44-45

The stone kingdom is the Kingdom of the Lord Jesus Christ, the Millennial Kingdom that crushes the iron, bronze, clay, silver, and gold. All these empires will exist at the last days. Does Babylon (Iraq), Persia (Iran), Greece (Greece & Turkey) and the other countries of the Ottoman Empire exist today? Yes. They will be destroyed at the Second Coming of Jesus Christ.

The stone kingdom grows into a mountain and consumes the earth. The millennial reign of the Lord Jesus Christ will fill the entire world. His kingdom will be inaugurated at His Second Coming at the end of the 7-year Tribulation.

The great image of Nebuchadnezzar's dream was a vision of successive empires that follow Babylon. The head of gold is Babylon, the chest and arms of silver Media-Persia, the belly and thighs of bronze Greece, the legs of iron represent the Islamic/Ottoman empires and the feet and toes are the final stage of the revived Islamic/Ottoman caliphate with a 10-nation confederacy. The Stone that smites the feet is the Lord Jesus Christ at his second coming. He will defeat the 10-nation confederacy as well as the others and set up his millennial kingdom that will fill the earth and reign for 1,000 years initially but will continue forever.

Chäptër Twä

Däniël's Fäur Bëästs

Daniel Chapter 7

Many years had passed since Daniel interpreted Nebuchadnezzar's dream. He is now serving under Belshazzar, Nebuchadnezzar's grandson. Daniel receives a vision of four great beasts.

*"Daniel spake and said, I saw in my vision by night, and, behold, the four winds of the heaven strove upon the great sea. And **four great beasts came up from the sea**, diverse one from another."* — Daniel 7:2-3

The great sea is the sea of humanity in the Middle East, not the Mediterranean. The four beasts are kingdoms that will arise in the Middle East.

*"**The first was like a lion**, and had eagle's wings: I beheld till the wings thereof were plucked, and it was lifted up from the earth, and made stand upon the feet as a man, and a man's heart was given to it."* — Daniel 7:4

*"And behold **another beast, a second, like to a bear**, and it raised up itself on one side, and it had three ribs in the mouth of it between the teeth of it: and they said thus unto it, Arise, devour much flesh."* — Daniel 7:5

9

*"After this I beheld, and lo **another, like a leopard**, which had upon the back of it **four wings of a fowl**; the beast had also **four heads**; and dominion was given to it."* — *Daniel 7:6*

*"After this I saw in the night visions, and behold a **fourth beast, dreadful and terrible**, and strong exceedingly; and it had great iron teeth: it **devoured and brake in pieces, and stamped the residue** with the feet of it: and it was **diverse from all the beasts** that were before it; and it had **ten horns**."* — *Daniel 7:7*

The fourth beast will conquer the previous three kingdoms.

Four Beasts:
1. Lion
2. Bear
3. Leopard
4. Dreadful Beast with 10 horns

*"I considered the horns, and, behold, there came up among them another **little horn**, before whom there were three of the first horns plucked up by the roots: and, behold, in this horn were eyes like the **eyes of man**, and a **mouth speaking great things**."* — *Daniel 7:8*

*"I beheld till the thrones were cast down, and the **Ancient of days did sit**, whose garment was white as snow, and the hair of his head like the pure wool: his throne was like the fiery flame, and his wheels as burning fire."* — *Daniel 7:9*

The "little horn" that arises from among the 10 horns of the dreadful fourth beast (kingdom) is the Antichrist. He is a man speaking great blasphemies.

Ancient of Days – God the Father sits in judgment of the beast kingdom and the Antichrist.

"A fiery stream issued and came forth from before him: thousand thousands ministered unto him, and ten thousand times ten thousand stood before him: the judgment was set, and the books were opened. I beheld then because of the voice of the great words which the horn spake: I beheld even till the beast was slain, and his body destroyed, and given to the burning flame. As concerning the rest of the beasts, they had their dominion taken away: yet their lives were prolonged for a season and time." — Daniel 7:10-12

The fourth beast kingdom is judged and cast into the burning flame (lake of fire) along with the little horn, the Antichrist.

"I saw in the night visions, and, behold, one like the Son of man came with the clouds of heaven, and came to the Ancient of days, and they brought him near before him. And there was given him dominion, and glory, and a kingdom, that all people, nations, and languages, should serve him: his dominion is an everlasting dominion, which shall not pass away, and his kingdom that which shall not be destroyed." — Daniel 7:13-14

This is a reference to the inauguration of the Millennial Reign of Jesus Christ, an everlasting dominion or kingdom. The Kingdom of the Lord Jesus Christ will fill this earth and continue for 1000 years and then for all eternity.

The Interpretation:

"I came near unto one of them that stood by, and asked him the truth of all this. So he told me, and made me know the interpretation of the things. These great beasts, which are four, are four kings, which shall arise out of the earth." — Daniel 7:16-17

Traditional Western Interpretation:
1. Lion — Babylon
2. Bear — Persia
3. Leopard — Greece
4. Terrible — Rome???

The question again, is Rome really the fourth Beast kingdom? What are the characteristics of the fourth Beast (v. 7)?

*"After this I saw in the night visions, and behold a fourth beast, **dreadful and terrible**, and **strong exceedingly**; and it had **great iron teeth**: it devoured and **brake in pieces**, and stamped the residue with the feet of it: and it was **diverse from all the beasts** that were before it; and it had **ten horns**."* — Daniel 7:7

Fourth Beast:
1. Dreadful and terrible, exceedingly strong
2. Great iron teeth
3. Devoured and broke in pieces the previous kingdoms
4. Diverse from the previous three
5. Has 10 horns (final form of the fourth kingdom)

Did Rome fulfill these requirements? No, as we saw in the previous chapter Rome wanted to tax, not destroy. Does Islam fulfill these requirements? Yes, Islam destroys other cultures by imposing Sharia law and enforcing the religion of Islam with the sword. Convert to Islam or die is their mantra.

The Fourth Beast:

*"Then I would know the truth of the **fourth beast**, which was **diverse from all the others, exceeding dreadful**, whose teeth were of **iron**, and his nails of **brass**; which devoured, **brake in pieces**, and stamped the residue with his feet; And of the **ten horns** that were in his head, and of the other which came up, and before whom three fell; even of*

12

*that horn that had **eyes**, and a **mouth that spake very great things**, whose look was more stout than his fellows. I beheld, and the **same horn made war with the saints**, and prevailed against them; Until the **Ancient of days** came, and **judgment** was given to the saints of the most High; and the time came that the **saints possessed the kingdom**." — Daniel 7:19-22*

The interpretation:

*"Thus he said, The fourth beast shall be the **fourth kingdom upon earth**, which shall be **diverse from all kingdoms, and shall devour the whole earth, and shall tread it down**, and break it in pieces. And the **ten horns out of this kingdom are ten kings** that shall arise: and **another shall rise after them**; and he shall be diverse from the first, and he shall subdue three kings. And he shall **speak great words against the most High**, and shall wear out the saints of the most High, and think to **change times and laws**: and they shall be given into his hand until a **time and times and the dividing of time**. But the **judgment shall sit**, and they shall take away his dominion, to consume and to destroy it unto the end. And the kingdom and dominion, and the greatness of the kingdom under the whole heaven, shall be given to the people of the **saints of the most High**, whose kingdom is an **everlasting kingdom**, and all dominions shall serve and obey him." — Daniel 7:23-27*

Here again, as in Daniel chapter two, we see the fourth beast *"**shall devour the whole earth**."* The word earth is the same as found in the previous phrase "fourth kingdom upon the earth." We know from previous usage of the word earth that the land mass of the Middle East is the intended meaning not the entire planet. Thus, the fourth kingdom in this vision will devour the entire Middle East. Did Rome devour the Middle East, no, but

Islam surely did and still controls the entire region today, except for Israel.

The fourth beast is the fourth and last gentile kingdom on earth because it is replaced by the Kingdom of the Most High. When we study the kingdoms of the seven headed beast in Revelation chapter 17, we will read that this last kingdom suffers a mortal wound just prior to the seven-year tribulation at the end of the age but is revived for a short time.

This fourth beast kingdom shall arise as a 10-nation confederation in the Middle East. From among the 10 kings shall arise another (little horn) and he is given dominion for 3 ½ years (a time, times and half a time), the last 3 ½ years of the 7-year tribulation.

The kingdom of the little horn (Antichrist) is destroyed and the Kingdom of the most High (Millennial Reign of Christ) given to the saints, the Jews.

Daniel Chapters 2 and 7 align perfectly:

Empire	Chapter 2	Chapter 7
Babylon	Head of Gold	Lion Beast
Media-Persia	Chest of Silver	Bear Beast
Greece	Belly and thighs of Brass	Leopard Beast
Islam	Legs of Iron & Feet of Clay	Terrible Beast
Caliphate	10 Toes-Kingdoms	10 Horns
Jesus' Millennial Kingdom	Stone Kingdom	Ancient of Days Son of Man

Chapter Three
The Ram and He Goat

Daniel Chapter 8

While serving under Belshazzar, Daniel receives another vision of a Ram and a He-Goat. Daniel is at the Persian palace at Shushan in the province of Elam (Iran).

"Then I lifted up mine eyes, and saw, and, behold, there stood before the river **a ram which had two horns**: *and the two horns were high; but one was higher than the other, and the higher came up last. I saw the ram pushing westward, and northward, and southward; so that no beasts might stand before him, neither was there any that could deliver out of his hand; but he did according to his will, and became great."—Daniel 8:3-4*

"And as I was considering, behold, an **he goat came from the west on the face of the whole earth**, *and touched not the ground: and the goat had a* **notable horn between his eyes**. *And he came to the ram that had two horns, which I had seen standing before the river, and ran unto him in the fury of his power. And I saw him come close unto the ram, and he was moved with choler against him, and* **smote the ram**, *and brake his two horns: and there was no power in the ram to stand before him, but he cast him down to the ground, and stamped upon him: and there was* **none that could deliver the ram out of his hand**." — Daniel 8:5-7*

15

The he-goat empire conquers the ram empire. Greece conquers Media-Persia.

*"Therefore the **he goat waxed very great**: and when he was strong, the **great horn was broken**; and for it came up **four notable ones** toward the four winds of heaven."* — Daniel 8:8

The King of the he-goat empire, Alexander the Great, is broken (dies) and four kings arise in his place.

*"And out of **one of them** came forth a **little horn**, which waxed **exceeding great**, toward the south, and toward the east, and toward the pleasant land."* — Daniel 8:9

Another little horn (king) arises:

*"And it **waxed great, even to the host of heaven; and it cast down some of the host and of the stars to the ground, and stamped upon them**. Yea, he magnified himself even to the prince of the host, and by him **the daily sacrifice was taken away**, and the **place of his sanctuary was cast down**. And an host was given him against the daily sacrifice by reason of transgression, and it cast down the truth to the ground; and it practised, and prospered. Then I heard one saint speaking, and another saint said unto that certain saint which spake, How long shall be the vision concerning the daily sacrifice, and the transgression of desolation, to give both the sanctuary and the host to be trodden under foot? And he said unto me, Unto **two thousand and three hundred days**; then shall the sanctuary be cleansed."* — Daniel 8:10-14

The little horn will prosper for almost 6 ½ years and then the temple will be cleansed.

The Interpretation:

*"And I heard a man's voice between the banks of Ulai, which called, and said, **Gabriel, make this man to understand the vision.** So he came near where I stood: and when he came, I was afraid, and fell upon my face: but he said unto me, **Understand, O son of man: for at the time of the end shall be the vision.** Now as he was speaking with me, I was in a deep sleep on my face toward the ground: but he touched me, and set me upright. And he said, Behold, I will make thee know what shall be in **the last end of the indignation; for at the time appointed the end shall be.** The ram which thou sawest having two horns are the **kings of Media and Persia**." — Daniel 8:16-20*

Understand, this vision is for the "***time of the end***" even though there will be a near term fulfillment. This concept of dual fulfillment is common in prophetic Scripture. The ram with two horns is the Media/Persian Empire. The empire of Media-Persia followed Babylon and ruled the region for about a century.

*"And the **rough goat is the king of Grecia:** and the great horn that is between his eyes is the **first king**." — Daniel 8:21*

The he goat is the Empire of Greece and the notable horn is Alexander the Great who died in 323 B.C.

*"Now that being broken, whereas four stood up for it, **four kingdoms shall stand up out of the nation, but not in his power.**" — Daniel 8:22*

After Alexander's death, the Grecian Empire was divided amongst his four generals:
1. Egypt, Libya, Palestine (under Ptolemy)
2. Asia Minor, Syria, Persia (under Seleucia)
3. Thrace, Bithynia, Pergamum (under Lysimachus)
4. Macedonia, Greece (under Cassander)

*"And in the **latter time of their kingdom**, when the transgressors are come to the full, a **king of fierce countenance, and understanding dark sentences**, shall stand up. And his power shall be mighty, but not by his own power: and **he shall destroy wonderfully, and shall prosper**, and practise, and shall destroy the mighty and the holy people. And through his policy also he shall **cause craft to prosper** in his hand; and he shall magnify himself in his heart, and **by peace shall destroy many**: he shall also **stand up against the Prince of princes**; but he shall be broken without hand."* — *Daniel 8:23-25*

A Little Horn, Antichrist, arises from one of the four notable horns with the following characteristics:

- Grows exceedingly great in the Middle East.
- Persecutes the saints (Jews).
- Removes the daily sacrifice from the Temple.
- Understands dark (occult) doctrines and sayings.
- Empowered by another (Satan).
- Destroys wonderfully (beyond one's own power).
- Deceit prospers (great deception).
- By peace shall destroy many (uses peace as a weapon).
- Stand up against the Prince of princes (Jesus Christ).
- Be destroyed without hand (not by man but God).

The *"king of fierce countenance"* arises in the latter times of the four kingdoms. He is the Antichrist, the Little Horn of chapters 7 and 8. There is a near term and an end time fulfillment of the "little horn" of chapter 8. The near-term fulfillment was Antiochus Epiphanies (170-163 B.C.) who is the primary type of the Antichrist.

In 167 B.C. Antiochus attacked Jerusalem killing thousands of Jews. He then entered the Temple and set up a statue of Zeus demanding all worship it or die. This is what Daniel and Jesus call the Abomination of Desolation. Judah Maccabee led the famous Maccabean Revolt defeating the

18

Seleucid Empire restoring autonomy to Israel. The war lasted 6 ½ years resulting in the cleansing of the Temple, Hanukkah, the Feast of Dedication.

During the 7-year Tribulation the Antichrist will perpetrate another Abomination of Desolation only to be defeated by the Lord Jesus Christ at His coming.

As you can see from the chart, in Daniel Chapters 2, 7 and 8 the Holy Spirit is progressively centering the focus from the general kingdoms of the end times down to the kingdom that will produce the Antichrist, the ancient area of Assyria. All of the kingdoms mentioned have their modern-day equivalent. Babylon is Iraq, Media is the Kurds, Persia is Iran, and Greece (Javan) is Turkey.

Empire	Chapter 2	Chapter 7	Chapter 8
Babylon	Head of Gold	Lion	
Media-Persia	Chest and Arms of Silver	Bear	Ram with two horns
Greece	Belly and Thighs of Bronze	Leopard	He-Goat with one great horn
Islamic Empire	Legs of Iron	Dreadful Beast	
Revived Islamic Caliphate	Feet of Iron and Clay 10 Toes	10 horns	Little Horn
Jesus' Millennial Reign	Stone Kingdom	Ancient of Days	

The little horn, Antichrist, will come from the geographical region of the Seleucid Empire.

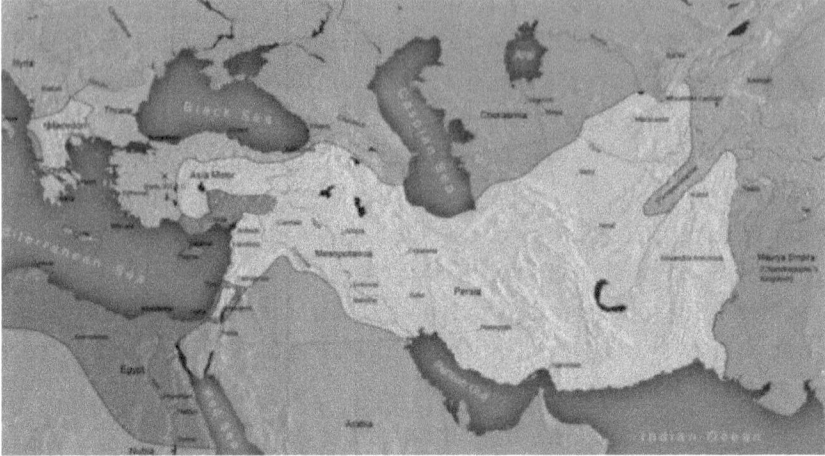

Pärt Twä

Thë Princë thät Shäll Cämë

Chäptër Fäur

Thë Sëvënty Wëëks Präphëcy

Daniel Chapter 9

The vision recorded by the Prophet Daniel in chapter 9:24-27 was given to him shortly after the conquering of Babylon by the Medes and Persians. Darius the Mede is now the ruler in Babylon. Daniel is aware of the prophecy of Jeremiah that the captivity in Babylon will be 70 years and the end of that period is drawing near.

"And this whole land shall be a desolation, and an astonishment; and ***these nations shall serve the king of Babylon seventy years.***" — *Jeremiah 25:11*

Daniel is praying asking the Lord what's next. Below is the Lord's answer.

"Seventy weeks are determined upon thy people and upon thy holy city, *to finish the transgression, and to make an end of sins, and to make reconciliation for iniquity, and to bring in everlasting righteousness, and to seal up the vision and prophecy, and to anoint* *the most Holy. Know therefore and understand, that from the going forth of the commandment to restore and to build Jerusalem unto the Messiah the Prince shall be seven weeks, and threescore and two weeks: the street shall be built again, and the wall, even in troublous times. And after threescore and two weeks shall Messiah be cut off, but not for himself: and the people of the prince that shall come shall destroy the city and the sanctuary; and the end thereof shall be with a flood, and unto the end of the war desolations are determined. And he shall confirm the covenant with many for one week: and in the midst of the week he shall cause the sacrifice and the oblation to cease, and for the overspreading of abominations he shall make it desolate, even until the consummation, and that determined shall be poured upon the desolate." — Daniel 9:24-27*

The 70 weeks vision is 70 sevens or seventy weeks of years not days. The period is 490 prophetic years of 360 days each. The vision is for Daniel's people the Jews and the holy city Jerusalem.

"Seventy weeks are determined upon thy people and upon thy holy city, *to finish the transgression, and to make an end of sins, and to make reconciliation for iniquity, and to bring in everlasting righteousness, and to seal up the vision and prophecy, and to anoint the most Holy." — Daniel 9: 24*

The prophecy is for 490 years and pertains solely to the Jews and Jerusalem. The purpose of the prophecy is to fulfill the following:

1. Finish the transgression.
2. Make an end of sins.
3. Make reconciliation for iniquity.
4. Bring in everlasting righteousness.
5. Seal up (complete) the vision and prophecy.
6. Anoint the most Holy (Place).

22

Have these six prophecies been fulfilled? No! Even though Jesus made reconciliation for iniquity on the cross, the Jews are yet to be reconciled to God. The others are also still yet unfulfilled. The Jews remain in the transgression of unbelief as they have not accepted Jesus as their Messiah; there is no end of sins; everlasting righteousness has not arrived; the prophecies of the last days are not yet fulfilled and the most Holy Place has not yet been anointed. In fact, at the time of this writing there is no Holy Place as the temple has yet to be re-built.

The beginning of the timeline:

*"Know therefore and understand, that **from the going forth of the commandment to restore and to build Jerusalem unto the Messiah the Prince shall be seven weeks, and threescore and two weeks: the street shall be built again, and the wall, even in troublous times.**"*
— Daniel 9: 25

When was the commandment to restore and build Jerusalem given? The command was given to Nehemiah in chapter 2 verse 17 of the book bearing his name. The command was given by Artaxerxes, King of Persia on March 14, 445 B.C. Nehemiah, saddened by the terrible state of ruin in Jerusalem, was given permission and materials to return to Jerusalem and rebuild the wall and the city.

There are three other commands recorded in the book of Ezra, but they all pertain to the rebuilding of the Temple, not the city and wall. What is the duration of this part of the 70 Weeks Prophecy?

7 weeks + 62 weeks = 69 weeks
69 weeks * 7-years per week = 483 years

The wall and the city were built during the first 7 weeks or 49-year period. This is recorded in the book of Nehemiah Chapters 3 – 8. After Jerusalem, the city wall and the Temple

23

were rebuilt the prophetic clock keeps ticking. What event marks the end of this 483-year period? Jesus, "Messiah the Prince" riding into Jerusalem upon a colt proclaiming himself Messiah of Israel. When did this happen? April 6, 32 A.D.

The definitive work on the chronology of Daniel 9 is "The Coming Prince" by Sir Robert Anderson. Below is a summary of the 483-year time period.

What is the math for the first 483 years?

1. 483 prophetic years * 360 days per prophetic year = 173,880 days.

2. 445 B.C to 32 A.D. = 445 + 32 – 1 = 476 years (subtract 1 year because there is no zero year between B.C. and A.D).

3. 476 years * 365 days = 173,740 days (Gregorian calendar).

4. 173,740 days + 24 days (March 14 to April 6) + 116 days for leap years = 173,880 days.

5. The 173,880 days in the prophecy are exactly the days from the command to rebuild Jerusalem unto Palm Sunday when Jesus presented himself as Messiah.

The first part of the prophecy is 483 years or 173,880 days. The number of days from March 14, 445 B.C. until April 6, 32 A.D. is exactly 173,880 days. Wow, the first section of 69 weeks or 483 years was fulfilled exactly to the day.

If this prophecy is so significant, did Jesus ever mention it? Yes.

*"And when he was come near, he beheld the city, and wept over it, Saying, If thou hadst known, even thou, **at least in this thy day**, the things which belong unto thy peace! but now they are hid from thine eyes. For the days shall come upon thee, that thine enemies shall cast a trench about thee, and compass thee round, and keep thee in on every side, And shall lay thee even with the ground, and thy children within thee; and they shall not leave in thee one stone upon another; because **thou knewest not the time of thy visitation**." — Luke 19: 41-44*

Shortly after arriving in Jerusalem and proclaiming himself the Messiah of the Jews, Jesus sat upon the Mount of Olives and wept over Jerusalem because they missed the day of their visitation, the day their "Messiah the Prince" would arrive. The Jews missed their Messiah because they did not study prophecy. The prophet Daniel told them the exact day of their Messiahs arrival.

After the 69 weeks (483 years) were completed, there is a gap v. 26. In the gap two events are listed.

1. Messiah is cut off (crucified)
2. People of the Prince that shall come shall destroy the city and temple (70 A.D.)

*"And **after threescore and two weeks shall Messiah be cut off**, but not for himself: and the **people of the prince that shall come shall destroy the city and the sanctuary**; and the end thereof shall be with a flood, and unto the end of the war desolations are determined." — Daniel 9: 26*

Messiah Jesus was cut off, crucified, not for himself but for the sin of the world. Had the Jews studied prophecy they would have known that their Messiah would come and die before the destruction of the second Temple.

25

Who were *"the people of the prince that shall come"*? The traditional understanding is that since the Roman Legions destroyed the Temple in 70 A.D. then the "people of the prince" are Romans (European Romans). Then what about the "prince" (Antichrist)? Well, he must be a Roman also. But is that true?

Traditional Position:
"The Antichrist will rise out of the heartland of the old Roman Empire, and he will be of Italian descent. Both Jerusalem and the Jewish Temple were destroyed by the Romans in 70 A.D. Therefore, according to Daniel, the Antichrist must be of Roman heritage." This is a quote from a popular Bible Prophecy teacher who has a program on a Christian television network.

Many Prophecy teachers believe that the Antichrist will be a European from the EU which they claim is the revived Roman Empire. Must you be European to be Roman?

The Apostle Paul was a Roman citizen but certainly was not European and certainly was not of Roman ancestry. He was born in Asia Minor, modern day Turkey.

*"Then the commander came and said to Paul, "Tell me, **are you a Roman**?" He said, **"Yes."** The commander answered, "With a large sum I obtained this citizenship." And Paul said, "But I was born a citizen. But Paul said, I am a man which am a Jew of Tarsus, a city in Cilicia, a citizen of no mean city..." — Acts 22:25-29*

Who are the "people" of the prince that shall come? Who invaded Jerusalem in 70 A.D.?

Joel Richardson makes the following observations from the works of Tacitus and Josephus in his video "Islam and the End Times" where he reveals the true identity of the "people of the prince that shall come."

"Early in this year Titus Caesar, who had been selected by his father to complete the subjugation of Judaea... He found in **Judaea** three legions, the 5th, the 10th, and the 15th, all old troops of Vespasian's. To these he added the 12th from **Syria**, and some men belonging to the 18th and 3rd, whom he had withdrawn from **Alexandria**... by a strong contingent of **Arabs**, who hated the Jews with the usual hatred of neighbors". — Tacitus, The Histories Book 5

Roman Legions:
Legion 5:	Macedonian
Legion 10:	Asia Minor / Syria / Arab
Legion 15:	Syria
Legion 12:	Asia Minor / Syria
Legion 18:	Egypt
Legion 3:	Egypt

Under Nero, just a few years earlier, Josephus commented on the Syrian dominance of the Roman Garrisons in Judea: "The greatest part of the Roman garrison **was raised out of Syria; and** being thus related to the Syrian part, they were ready to assist it." — Josephus, The Wars of The Jews, Book 2, Chapter 13

"Malchus also, the **king of Arabia**, sent a thousand horsemen, besides five thousand footmen..." — Josephus, The Wars of The Jews, Book 3, Chapter 4

"...the **multitude of the Arabians, with the Syrians,** cut up those that came as supplicants, and searched their bellies. Nor does it seem to me that any misery befell the Jews that was more terrible than this, since in one night's time about two thousand of these deserters were thus dissected." — Josephus, The Wars of The Jews, Book 5, Chapter 13

"Moreover, do the **Arabians and Syrians** now first of all begin to govern themselves as they please, and to indulge their appetites in a foreign war, and then, out of their barbarity in murdering men, and out of their hatred to the Jews, get it ascribed to the Romans?" — Josephus, The Wars of The Jews, Book 5, Chapter 13

The Roman garrisons that destroyed the Temple and the city of Jerusalem were comprised primarily of locals from the nearby regions. They were Syrians, Turks and Arabs that hated the Jews and were more than eager to destroy their holy city. But what about the Temple; was Rome responsible for the destruction of one of the eight wonders of the ancient world? Josephus gives us definite clues as to the position of Titus and Caesar.

"And now a certain person came running to Titus, and told him of this fire... whereupon he rose up in great haste, and, as he was, ran to the holy house, in order to have a stop put to the fire... Then did Caesar, both by calling to the soldiers that were fighting, with a loud voice, and by giving a signal to them with his right hand, order them to quench the fire."— *Josephus, The Wars of the Jews, Book 6, Chapter 4*

"Titus supposing what the fact was, that **the house itself might yet be saved, he came in haste and endeavored to persuade the soldiers to quench the fire**... yet were the regards they had for Caesar, and their dread of him who forbade them, not as hard as their passion and their hatred of the Jews, and a certain vehement inclination to fight them, too hard for them also... And thus was the holy house burnt down, without Caesar's approval." — Josephus, The Wars of the Jews, Book 6, Chapter 4

Syrians, Arabs, and Turks of the 10th Roman legion destroyed the Temple in 70 A.D., not European Romans. The "people of the prince that shall come" are Syrians, Turks, and Arabs. The destruction of the Temple in Jerusalem was done without permission or consent of Titus or Caesar.

The "prince that shall come" (the Antichrist) will be from the geographical area of ancient Assyria. As we shall see in Part Three, he is actually called "the Assyrian" several times in Scripture.

The Last 7-years:

As of this writing, only 483 years or 69 weeks of Daniel's prophecy have been completed. One week, the 70th week remains to be fulfilled. This one remaining week or 7-years is what we commonly call the 7-year Tribulation.

*"And **he shall confirm the covenant with many for one week**: and in the midst of the week he shall cause the sacrifice and the oblation to cease, and for the overspreading of abominations he shall make it desolate, even until the consummation, and that determined shall be poured upon the desolate." – Daniel 9: 27*

The "**he**" references the previous "prince that shall come" in v. 26. He is the Antichrist. He will confirm a 7-year covenant or treaty with Israel and her surrounding nations. To confirm means to bind up anything broken, to make firm, to strengthen. The Antichrist will confirm an existing treaty.

Currently, the only seven-year treaty signed by Israel is the Oslo Accords signed in 1993 by President Bill Clinton, Prime Minister Yitzhak Rabin, and Yasser Arafat at the public ceremony in Washington D.C. However, the U.N. is presently (2023) working on a 7-year agreement to complete the Sustainable Development Goals by 2030.

The fulfillment of this last week and the confirmation of the 7-year treaty is yet future. The confirmation of the treaty will begin the 7-year tribulation. Could the confirmation of the Oslo Accords begin the 7-year tribulation, very possibly? Most would think this a good thing; someone finally bringing peace to the Middle East. But remember, the Antichrist comes on the scene proclaiming peace; by peace he will destroy many. Also, part of this covenant will be the rebuilding of the temple in Jerusalem and the re-establishment of the covenant of Moses complete with priesthood and animal sacrifices, more on that later.

Chäptër Fivë

The Willful King

Picture of the Antichrist - Daniel Ch. 11 & 12

Daniel Chapter 11 portrays the confrontations starting about 550 B.C. with Darius king of Persia through Antiochus Epiphanies king of Syria 170 B.C. Our study will center on Antiochus as he is a type of the Antichrist to come. Antiochus Epiphanies, the Seleucid king of the north, fought many battles with the king of the south, Egypt. As we will see, he is a profound type of the Antichrist. Looking at Antiochus we can see some of the characteristics of the Antichrist.

Characteristics of Antiochus Epiphanies:
1. Vile person and a Liar.
2. Comes in peaceably.
3. Obtain kingdom by flatteries.
4. Work deceitfully (deceit is his MO).
5. Become strong with a small group of people.
6. Scatter the prey, take spoil and riches.
7. Takes away the daily sacrifice in the Temple.
8. Perpetrates the Abomination of desolation.

The Willful King v. 36-45:
1. Does according to his own will not God's.
2. Exalts himself above every god.
3. Speaks blasphemies against the one true God.
4. Does not regard the pagan gods of his fathers.
5. Nor the pagan desire of women.
6. Honors the god of fortresses (war).
7. Divides the land of Israel for gain.

31

8. Jordan will escape his control.
9. Will conquer Egypt.
10. Comes to his end with no help.

Chapter 12 continues with the archangel Michael standing up for the nation of Israel during their time of trouble, the last half of the 7-year tribulation. Only those whose names are written in the book of life will be delivered.

*"And at that time shall Michael stand up, the great prince **which standeth for the children of thy people**: and there shall be a **time of trouble**, such as never was since there was a nation even to that same time: and at that time **thy people shall be delivered, every one that shall be found written in the book**."* — Daniel 12:1

How long shall it be to the end of these wonders?

*"And one said to the man clothed in linen, which was upon the waters of the river, **How long shall it be to the end of these wonders?** And I heard the man clothed in linen, which was upon the waters of the river, when he held up his right hand and his left hand unto heaven, and sware by him that liveth forever **that it shall be for a time, times, and an half**; and when he shall have accomplished to scatter the power of the holy people, all these things shall be finished."* — *Daniel 12:6-7*

Time, times, and half a time = 3 ½ years.

When the Antichrist accomplishes the breaking up of the people of Israel it will be finished. None of the wicked shall understand but the wise will understand. This 3 ½ year period is the last half of the 7-year tribulation (70th week of Daniel's Prophecy). Jesus said in Matthew 24 that this period would be the greatest period of tribulation, judgment and destruction that would ever come upon the earth.

*"For then shall be great tribulation, such as was **not since the beginning of the world to this time, no, nor ever shall be.**"* — Matthew 24:21

I cover this in detail in the chapter on the Gospel of Matthew.

"And I heard, but I understood not: then said I, O my Lord, what shall be the end of these things? And he said, Go thy way, Daniel: for the words are closed up and sealed till the time of the end. Many shall be purified, and made white, and tried; but the wicked shall do wickedly: and none of the wicked shall understand; but the wise shall understand. ***And from the time that the daily sacrifice shall be taken away, and the abomination that maketh desolate set up, there shall be a thousand two hundred and ninety days.*** *Blessed is he that waiteth, and cometh to the thousand three hundred and five and thirty days. But go thou thy way till the end be: for thou shalt rest, and stand in thy lot at the end of the days."* — Daniel 12:8-13

From when the Antichrist stops the daily sacrifice in the Temple and perpetrates the abomination of desolation until the end of the Tribulation is 1260 days. Following the return of Jesus Christ, the Temple will be cleansed for 30 days giving the 1290 days. Blessed is he that lives to the 1335 day because he has survived the tribulation and the judgment of the nations. He will enter the Millennial Kingdom reserved for the saints of the Lord, Israel.

    1260 days = last 3 ½ years of the tribulation
    30 days = cleansing of the temple of the abomination
    45 days = finish the judgment of the nations

Part Three

Antichrist the Assyrian

Chapter Six
Micah Chapter Five

The Assyrian Antichrist

Most Christians are familiar with Micah 5:2.

*"But thou, **Bethlehem Ephratah**, though thou be little among the thousands of **Judah**, yet out of thee shall he come forth unto me that is to be **ruler in Israel**; whose goings forth have been from of old, from everlasting."*

This is the scripture proclaiming the Messiah's birth in Bethlehem of Judea. But let's continue reading.

*"Therefore **will he give them up, until the time that she which travaileth hath brought forth: then the remnant of his brethren shall return** unto the children of Israel." — Micah 5:3*

When the rulers of Israel in Matthew 12 rejected Jesus, "he gave them up" until when — Until "she" (Israel) which travails (7-year Tribulation) hath brought forth (The redeemed nation of Israel in the Land) and "the remnant of his (Jesus)

35

brethren shall return." Israel shall be restored to the kingdom at the second coming of Jesus Christ.

"And he shall stand and feed in the strength of the LORD, in the majesty of the name of the LORD his God; and they shall abide: for **now shall he be great unto the ends of the earth.**"— *Micah 5: 4*

At the Second Coming Jesus will stand in the strength of God, the majesty of His name and Israel shall be rescued, for Jesus will be great in all the world.

"And **this man shall be the peace**, *when the* **Assyrian shall come into our land***: and when he shall tread in our palaces, then shall we raise against him seven shepherds, and eight principal men."* — *Micah 5:5*

Jesus is peace, the Prince of Peace. The Assyrian Antichrist will invade Israel, tread the palaces and capture the Temple. Israel will have 7 allies, and 8 military leaders. Not everyone on earth will be initially under the control of the Antichrist. Here 7 nations will fight against him.

"And **they shall waste the land of Assyria** *with the sword, and the* **land of Nimrod** *in the entrances thereof: thus shall he deliver us from* **the Assyrian**, *when he cometh into our land, and when he treadeth within our borders."* — *Micah 5:6*

The Lord will use these allies to destroy the land of Assyria and Iraq. He shall deliver Israel from the hand of the Antichrist "when he cometh into our land".

"And the **remnant of Jacob** *shall be in the* **midst of many people** *as a dew from the LORD, as the showers upon the grass, that tarrieth not for man, nor waiteth for the sons of men."* — *Micah 5:7*

*"And the **remnant of Jacob shall be among the Gentiles** in the midst of many people as a lion among the beasts of the forest, as a young lion among the flocks of sheep: who, if he go through, both treadeth down, and teareth in pieces, and none can deliver."* — Micah 5:8

*"Thine hand shall be lifted up upon thine adversaries, and **all thine enemies shall be cut off.**"* — Micah 5:9

*"And it shall come to pass in **that day**, saith the LORD, that I will cut off thy horses out of the midst of thee, and I will destroy thy chariots: And I will **cut off the cities of thy land**, and throw down all thy strong holds: And I will cut off witchcrafts out of thine hand; and thou shalt have no more soothsayers: Thy graven images also will I cut off, and thy standing images out of the midst of thee; and thou shalt no more worship the work of thine hands. And I will pluck up thy groves out of the midst of thee: so will I destroy thy cities. **And I will execute vengeance in anger and fury upon the heathen, such as they have not heard.**"* — Micah 5:10-15

At the Second Coming, the Lord Jesus will cut off (kill and destroy) the Assyrian and the enemies of Israel and their cities and their false religion (Islam).

Chapter Seven

The King of Babylon

The king of Babylon is a type of the Antichrist. He is the mystery of iniquity when Lucifer becomes a man.

*"That thou shalt take up this proverb against the **king of Babylon**, and say, How hath the oppressor ceased! the golden city ceased! The LORD hath broken the staff of the wicked, and the sceptre of the rulers. He who smote the people in wrath with a continual stroke, he that ruled the nations in anger, is persecuted, and none hindereth. The whole earth is at rest, and is quiet: they break forth into singing. Yea, the fir trees rejoice at thee, and the cedars of Lebanon, saying, Since thou art laid down, no feller is come up against us. **Hell from beneath is moved for thee to meet thee at thy coming: it stirreth up the dead for thee,** even all the chief ones of the earth; it hath raised up from their thrones all the kings of the nations. All they shall speak and say unto thee, Art thou also become weak as we? art thou become like unto us? Thy pomp is brought down to the grave, and the noise of thy viols: the worm is spread under thee, and the worms cover thee. **How art thou fallen from heaven, O Lucifer, son of the morning! how art thou cut down to the ground, which didst weaken the nations!"* — Isaiah 14:4-12*

Hell is moved and stirred up to meet the King of Babylon at his coming. He is equated in verse 12 to Lucifer, Satan, the devil. We know that hell was created for Satan and the angels that rebelled against God. Many souls are presently in hell, but Satan has never been there. Even though Satan is a defeated foe he is yet to be permanently confined to hell. He still has access to heaven because he is the accuser that stands before God accusing the brethren. He has not set one foot in hell, but the day is coming soon when he will be set in chains and taken to hell. This is why hell is stirred up. They are getting excited about finally seeing the one partly responsible for them being in hell. However, this will not be a glorious homecoming. Those in hell are fuming mad and furious with Satan. Satan's time in hell will be one of complete humiliation and scorn. They would rip him apart if they could.

*"For thou hast said in thine heart, **I will** ascend into heaven, **I will** exalt my throne above the stars of God: **I will** sit also upon the mount of the congregation, in the sides of the north: **I will** ascend above the heights of the clouds; **I will** be like the most High. **Yet thou shalt be brought down to hell, to the sides of the pit.**"* — Isaiah 14:13-15

*"They that see thee shall narrowly look upon thee, and consider thee, saying, **Is this the man that made the earth to tremble, that did shake kingdoms;** That made the world as a wilderness, and destroyed the cities thereof; that opened not the house of his prisoners?"* — Isaiah 14: 16-17

When did Lucifer become a man? He becomes a man when he indwells the Antichrist during the last 3 ½ years of the tribulation. The King of Babylon just as the Assyrian are titles of the Antichrist.

Nebuchadnezzar was the first important king of Babylon, and he is a type of the Antichrist. We read in Daniel chapter 3 that he sets up a golden image in the plain of Dura and forces all to worship the image. Not happy with the plan of God revealed to him in Daniel chapter 2 he tries to thwart the will of God by creating his own image and worship. This is exactly what the Antichrist will do in the temple at the middle of the 7-year tribulation. Also, in Daniel chapter 4 Nebuchadnezzar is given the heart of a beast for 7-years symbolic of the Antichrist's 7-year rise to power and reign.

The Assyrian:

*"I will **crush the Assyrian in my land; on my mountains I will trample him down**. His yoke will be taken from my people, and his burden removed from their shoulders. This is the plan determined for the whole world; this is the hand stretched out over all nations. For Yahweh Almighty has purposed, and who can thwart him? His hand is stretched out, and who can turn it back?"* — Isaiah 14:25-27

*"**Woe to the Assyrian**, the rod of my anger, in whose hand is the club of my wrath! I send him against a godless nation, I dispatch him against a people who anger me, to seize loot and snatch plunder, and to trample them down like mud in the streets... 12 **When the Lord has finished all his work against Mount Zion and Jerusalem, he will say, 'I will punish the king of Assyria** for the willful pride of his heart and the haughty look in his eyes. ...16 Therefore, the Lord, Yahweh Almighty, will send a wasting disease upon his sturdy warriors; under his pomp a fire will be kindled like a blazing flame. The Light of Israel will become a fire, their Holy One a flame; in a **single day** it will burn and consume his thorns and his briers."* — Isaiah 10:5-6,12-13, 16-17

Isaiah clearly defines the Antichrist as "the Assyrian" (eastern Turkey, Iraq, Syria, Jordan and Egypt). Also, in chapter 30 we find the Assyrian again.

*"Behold, the name of the LORD cometh from far, **burning with his anger**, and the burden thereof is heavy: his lips are full of in-dignation, and **his tongue as a devouring fire**: And his breath, as an overflowing stream, shall reach to the midst of the neck, to **sift the***

*nations with the sieve of vanity: and there shall be a bridle in the jaws of the people, causing them to err. Ye shall have a song, as in the night when a holy solemnity is kept; and gladness of heart, as when one goeth with a pipe to come into the mountain of the LORD, to the mighty One of Israel. And the LORD shall cause his glorious voice to be heard, and shall shew the lighting down of his arm, with the **indignation of his anger**, and with the **flame of a devouring fire**, with scattering, and **tempest**, and **hailstones**. For through the voice of the LORD shall the **Assyrian be beaten down, which smote with a rod**." — Isaiah 30:27-31*

Both Micah and Isaiah identify the coming Antichrist as originating from the ancient land of Assyria, not Europe as many erroneously believe.

Characteristics of the Antichrist – review Daniel 7:
1. Arises from among 10 kings.
2. Speaks great things (blasphemies).
3. Judged and destroyed by the Ancient of Days.
4. More stout that the other kings.
5. Made war with the saints and prevailed.
6. Changes the times and laws.
7. Reigns for 3 ½ years.

Daniel 8:
1. Grows exceedingly great.
2. Persecutes the saints.
3. Removes the daily sacrifice.
4. Understands dark sentences.
5. Empowered by another (Satan).
6. Destroys wonderfully.
7. Deceit prospers.
8. By peace shall destroy many.
9. Stand up against the Prince of princes (Jesus).
10. Be destroyed without hand.

Daniel 11:
1. Vile person.
2. Come in peaceably.
3. Obtain kingdom by flatteries.
4. Work deceitfully.
5. Become strong with a small people.
6. Scatter the prey, spoil and riches.
7. Liar.
8. Takes away the daily sacrifice.
9. Abomination of desolation.

The Willful King v. 36-45:
1. Do according to his own will.
2. Exalt himself above every god.
3. Speak blasphemies against God.
4. Not regard the gods of his fathers.
5. Nor the desire of women.
6. Honor the god of fortresses (war).
7. Divide the land for gain.
8. Jordan will escape his control.
9. Will control Egypt.
10. Come to his end with no help.

Interesting verses: Some use these verses to hint that the Antichrist is a homosexual Jew; nothing could be further from the truth.

"Neither shall he regard the God (Elohiym, gods plural) of his fathers, nor the desire of women, nor regard any god (elowahh, false god) for he shall magnify himself above all." — Daniel 11:37

*"But in his estate shall he honour the **God** (elowahh, false god) of forces: and a god whom his fathers knew not shall he honour with gold, and silver, and with precious stones, and pleasant things" — Daniel 11:38*

Paraphrase of Daniel 11: 37-38: Neither shall the Antichrist regard the **pagan gods of his fathers,** nor the **pagan desires of women,** nor regard any false god: for he shall magnify himself above all. The Antichrist honors no god but himself only. But in his official capacity and office shall he honor the false god of war: and a false god whom his father's knew not shall he honor with gold, and silver, and with precious stones, and pleasant things. He will honor this god because it is the god of his followers.

The phrase 'of forces' is the Hebrew word *ma'owz* meaning fortress, forces, strength or strong. When *ma'owz* is translated into Arabic it is *Al-mu'izz.* Al-mu'izz is one of the ninety-nine names of Allah, the god of Islam. Allah Al-mu'izz is the god of strength, power and might.

The Holy Spirit has revealed, through the prophet Daniel, the name of the false pagan god of the Antichrist, Allah, the moon god, the god of Islam.

Ezekiel calls the Antichrist the "King of Tyre". When was the king of Tyre ever in the Garden of Eden? Here we have a king, a man and Satan all in one person.

*"Son of man, say unto the **prince of Tyrus**, Thus saith the Lord GOD; Because thine heart is lifted up, and thou hast said, **I am a God, I sit in the seat of God**, in the midst of the seas; yet **thou art a man**, and not God, though thou set thine heart as the heart of God: Behold, thou art wiser than Daniel; there is no secret that they can hide from thee: With thy wisdom and with thine understanding thou hast gotten thee riches, and hast gotten gold and silver into thy treasures: They shall bring thee down to the pit, and thou shalt die the deaths of them that are slain in the midst of the seas... Son of man, take up a lamentation upon the king of Tyrus, and say unto him, Thus saith the Lord GOD; **Thou sealest up the sum, full of wisdom, and perfect in beauty.** Thou hast been in **Eden the garden***

44

*of God; every precious stone was thy covering, the sardius, topaz, and the diamond, the beryl, the onyx, and the jasper, the sapphire, the emerald, and the carbuncle, and gold: the workmanship of thy tabrets and of thy pipes was prepared in thee in the day that thou wast created. Thou art the **anointed cherub that covereth**; and I have set thee so: **thou wast upon the holy mountain of God**; thou hast walked up and down in the midst of the stones of fire. Thou wast perfect in thy ways from the day that thou wast created, till iniquity was found in thee… Thine heart was lifted up because of thy beauty, thou hast corrupted thy wisdom by reason of thy brightness: **I will cast thee to the ground, I will lay thee before kings, that they may behold thee.***"
— *Ezekiel 28:2-17*

As you can see, the Antichrist is a unique individual. Just as Jesus is the mystery of godliness, God manifest in the flesh. The Antichrist is the mystery of iniquity, Satan manifest in the flesh. Satan is a defeated foe but not yet a destroyed foe. He still has much power and will unleash it during the Tribulation.

Chapter Eight
The Mahdi Antichrist

The Apostle John writes:

"Who is a liar but he that denieth that Jesus is the Christ? **He is Antichrist, that denieth the Father and the Son.** *Whosoever* **denieth the Son, the same hath not the Father:** *(but) he that acknowledgeth the Son hath the Father also." — 1 John 22-23*

"And **every spirit that confesseth not that Jesus Christ is come in the flesh is not of God: and this is that spirit of Antichrist,** *whereof ye have heard that it should come; and even now already is it in the world." — 1 John 4:3*

"For many **deceivers** *are entered into the world,* **who confess not that Jesus Christ is come in the flesh.** *This is a deceiver and* **an Antichrist."** *— 2 John 1:7*

The spirit of Antichrist will deny the Father-Son relationship specifically that Jesus Christ is the one and only begotten Son of God. He will deny that Jesus, the Son of God, came to this world in the flesh. The only religion that fulfills this is Islam. Islam, in their Quran, deny that Jesus is the Son of God.

*"**No son did Allah beget**, nor is there any god along with Him:"* Quran 23:91

*"It is **not befitting** to (the majesty of) Allah that He should beget a son." Quran 19:35*

As you can read, according to Islam, Allah has no son. Islam denies the Son of God therefore they have not the Father either. The creed of Islam, the Shahada, states "There is no god but Allah and Mohammed is his messenger." Islam acknowledges Jesus as a prophet, but not the Son of God.

We have heard Muslims use the phrase "Allahu Akbar" and the moderate apologists say that it simply means "god is great." That is incorrect; the phrase means "Allah is the greatest." This is a direct assault on the true God of the Bible, the God of Abraham, Isaac, and Jacob.

Islam, the religion of Antichrist, is empowered by an Antichrist spirit. Be very careful of those ignorant politicians and preachers that say Christians, Jews and Muslims all worship the same God. This is a bald-faced lie. Never accept any instruction or teaching from such a false teacher.

Do Muslims have a Messiah figure whose arrival is greatly anticipated? Yes. He is called the Mahdi (al-Mahdi). He is also called the 12th Imam by the Shiite fundamentalists. The leadership of Iran are "twelvers" that eagerly await the appearance of the 12th Imam, the Mahdi. They believe when the Mahdi comes, he will spread Islam throughout the world and reign from Jerusalem, not Mecca. Why Jerusalem, even the devil knows Jerusalem is the holy city of the one true God.

Does the Bible speak of any such character as the Mahdi that will arise in the last days? Yes, he has many names but commonly referred to as the Antichrist.

The following is a comparison of the Biblical Antichrist and the Islamic Mahdi.

1. **Both deny the Trinity and the Cross.** Throughout the world Muslims are anti-Trinity, anti-Son, anti-Crucifixion, and anti-God-in-the-flesh. To attribute a trinity to Allah is blasphemy in Islam. "They blaspheme who say that Allah is the third of three." (Quran 5:73)

2. **Both deny the Father and the Son.** Nowhere in Scripture does the Antichrist claim to be the son of God. He claims to be God. We have already seen that Allah has no son.

3. **Both Blaspheme.** Both will speak great blasphemy against the God of the Bible and Jesus.

4. **Both are called the Deceiver.** 2 John 1:7 states that the Antichrist is a deceiver. In the Quran, Allah has a name Khayrul-Makireen which literally means "The Greatest of all Deceivers." (Quran 3:54)

5. **Both claim to be Messiah.** Matthew tells us in 24:24 that false Christ's will come. The Mahdi will bring peace to the earth by uniting everyone under the banner of Islam.

6. **Both Kingdoms suffer a "Head Wound".** Revelation 13:2-3 one of the kingdoms suffers a mortal head wound. On March 3, 1924 the office of the caliph of the Ottoman Empire was abolished. This was akin to some authority abolishing the office of the Pope. The Muslim world is being called to awake from its darkness and resume its destiny.

7. **Both work False Miracles.** 2 Thess 2:8-9 clearly state the Antichrist will operate with all power, signs and false wonders. In Islamic tradition Allah gives the Mahdi power over the wind and rain, supernatural control over nature.

8. **Both ride a White Horse.** The Antichrist is revealed in the first seal of Revelation chapter 6 riding a white horse going forth to conquer. Muslim authors Muhammad Ibn Izzat and Muhammad Arif state that "It is clear that this man is the Mahdi who will ride the white horse and judge by the Quran…"

9. **Both Attempt to Change the Law.** Daniel 7:25 declares that the Antichrist will try to change the set times and laws. The Mahdi will attempt to institute Sharia Law and force the use of the Muslim calendar.

10. **Both Rule over Ten Entities**. As we have seen, the Antichrist rules a 10-nation kingdom. In the plan for the return of the Caliphate, the Caliph will rule over a 10-member cabinet of assistant caliphs.

11. **Both are a Source of Death and War**. The Antichrist destroys many through a false peace. One of the 99 names for Allah is Al-Mumeet meaning "the one who possesses the power of death, causer of death, the slayer, and the taker of life or the destroyer of life."

12. **Both use Military Force**. The second horseman of revelation chapter 6 is the red horse of war. Muslim author Harun Yahya states "The Mahdi will invade all the places between the East and West."

13. **Both Condone Rape**. The battle against Jerusalem is described by Zechariah in chapter 14:2 "Behold, the day of the Lord cometh, and the spoil shall be divided in the midst of thee. For I will gather all nations against Jerusalem to battle; and the city shall be taken, and the houses rifled, and the women ravished." Today in Europe, Australia and elsewhere, rape is blamed by Muslim clerics on the woman for not wearing a headscarf.

14. **Both usher in a 7-year Peace Treaty**. In Daniel 9:27 the Antichrist confirms a seven-year peace treaty with Israel and surrounding nations. Islamic tradition states "The Mahdi will fill the earth with equity and justice as it was filled with oppression and tyranny, and he will rule for seven years."

15. **Both Destroy by Peace**. "By peace he will destroy many." (Daniel 8:25) Throughout the history of Islam, the hudna has been used to deceive the enemy. The hudna is a peace agreement made with an enemy to gain concessions, rearm, and prepare for another attack. The purpose of an Islamic peace treaty is to give them time to get the upper hand. In 1994 Yasser Arafat declared to a Muslim crowd at a mosque in Johannesburg (not

realizing that he was being taped) that the Oslo Accords were merely a way to facilitate his Jihad against Israel.

16. **Both will lead a Turkish-Iranian Invasion.** Ezekiel 38-39 describes a Turkish-Iranian invasion lead by Gog (Antichrist). Islamic author Abdul Rahman Wahabi, in his book *The Day of Wrath* states "The final battle will be waged by Muslim faithful's coming on the backs of horses carrying black banners. They will stand on the east side of the Jordan River and will wage war that the earth has never seen before. The true Messiah who is the Islamic Mahdi will defeat Europe; will lead this army of Seljuks (Turks). He will preside over the world from Jerusalem because Mecca would have been destroyed."

17. **Both desire Israel's Destruction.** Zechariah 14 describes the destruction of Israel wherein two thirds of the Jews are killed. In the previous quote we see the Mahdi ruling from Jerusalem.

The coming Islamic Messiah, the Mahdi, is the Biblical Antichrist. The above 17 "coincidences" just scratch the surface. Keep your eyes on the Middle East, he will arise soon. But remember, we are looking for Jesus Christ, not the Antichrist.

Part Four

The Coming Wars

Chapter Nine

The Next Big One

There are two major wars predicted in Scripture for the Last Days. Both obviously are Middle Eastern wars centered on Israel and Jerusalem. There are other minor wars and skirmishes as we have seen over the past 60 years including the continuing conflict with Hamas in Gaza. Hezbollah, Al-Qaeda, the Muslim Brotherhood, and ISIS are sure to join the fray at some time in the future. Jesus said there will be wars and rumors of wars right up to His second coming.

The next big war is with Israel's surrounding neighbors. This war is commonly referred to as the Zechariah Ch. 12 war or the Psalm 83 war.

*"Keep not thou silence, O God: hold not thy peace, and be not still, O God. For, lo, **thine enemies make a tumult**: and they that hate thee have **lifted up the head**. They have **taken crafty counsel against thy people**, and consulted against thy hidden ones." – Psalm 83:1-3*

The psalmist is asking the Lord to not be still, to not be at peace but to rise up against the enemies of Israel. Israel's enemies are in a tumult against her as we see every day in the news. They have "lifted up the head" in prideful arrogance boasting about their false god Allah and blaspheming the God of the Bible. They take counsel and make plans for the destruction of Israel and the Jew. If you listen to the leaders and Imam's throughout the Middle East, they continually call for the destruction of Israel. They shout, "kill the Jew, kill the Christian."

*"They have said, Come, and **let us cut them off from being a nation**; that the name of Israel may be no more in remembrance. For they have consulted together with one consent: they are confederate against thee: The tabernacles of **Edom**, and the **Ishmaelites**; of **Moab**, and the **Hagarenes**; **Gebal**, and **Ammon**, and **Amalek**; the **Philistines** with the inhabitants of **Tyre**;" - Psalm 83:4-7*

These nations want not only to destroy Israel but to wipe out any evidence that Israel ever existed. This confederation of nations against Israel begins with Edom and the Ishmaelites which are southern Jordan and Saudi Arabia. Moab is central Jordan. The Hagarines refer to Egypt, the country of Hagar and possibly Arabia as that is where her and Ishmael settled. Gebal and Ammon complete the peoples of Jordan. Amalek, the Philistines and Tyre are the coastal regions from the Sinai to and including Lebanon.

*"**Assur** also is joined with them: they have holpen the children of Lot. Selah." - Psalm 83:8-11*

Assur is a reference to Assyria which would include western Iraq, Syria. The children of Lot are Moab and Ammon (Gen 19:36-38), Assyria was their right arm of military strength (holpen). Where are all these nations on a map of the Middle East? They are Israel's immediate neighbors as we see on the following map. The countries involved in this war against Israel are Jordan, Saudi Arabia, Egypt, Lebanon, Syria, and Iraq. It is interesting that Tyre and the Philistines are mentioned as they are the regions of Hezbollah and Hamas.

"Do unto them as unto **the Midianites***; as to Sisera, as to Jabin, at the brook of Kison: Which perished at Endor: they became as dung for the earth. Make their nobles like Oreb, and like Zeeb: yea, all their princes as Zebah, and as Zalmunna" - Psalm 83:9-11*

The psalmist asks the Lord to do unto those nations that are planning to attack Israel as He did unto the Midianites; Sisera, Jabin, Oreb, Zeeb, Zebah and Zalmuna. These were kings of Midian, northwestern Arabia. We read about these kings in the book of Judges Chapters 7 & 8 where Gideon defeats these kings that are attacking Israel. The story of Gideon is remarkably interesting as God takes a young man hiding in the winepress and makes him a great warrior. With an army of only 300 men, he defeats the huge army of Midian. Actually, God defeats the Midianites, Gideon's men just made a lot of noise.

This war with Israel's surrounding neighbors is also described in Zechariah Ch. 12.

*"Behold, I will make **Jerusalem a cup of trembling** unto all **the people round about, when they shall be in the siege both against Judah and against Jerusalem**. And in that day will I make Jerusalem a **burdensome stone** for all people: all that burden themselves with it shall be cut in pieces, though all the people of the earth be gathered together against it." - Zechariah 12:2-3*

Jerusalem is made a "cup of trembling," a cup of drunkenness to all her nearby neighbors. They are seemingly drunk and obsessed with taking control of Jerusalem and wrestling the holy city from the Jews. It is also made a "burdensome stone" to all those that try to change the city boundaries. Those that try will be "cut in pieces", killed for their unholy actions.

*"In that day will I make the governors of Judah like an **hearth of fire among the wood, and like a torch of fire in a sheaf; and they shall devour all the people round about**, on the right hand and on the left: and Jerusalem shall be inhabited again in her own place, even in Jerusalem. ... In that day shall the LORD defend the inhabitants of Jerusalem; and he that is feeble among them at that day shall be as David; and the house of David shall be as God, as the angel of the LORD before them." - Zechariah 12:6, 8*

As a "hearth of fire", a large fireplace, consumes much wood, Israel will consume her surrounding neighbors in this coming war. A "torch of fire" will quickly consume a sheaf of straw. This is how quick and decisive this war will transpire. The afore mentioned countries will be decimated by the IDF. This war is a great victory for Israel as they "devour all the people round about." But the next war, the Gog/Magog war, has a much different scenario perpetrated against Israel.

Chapter Ten

Ezekiel Chapters Thirty Eight and Thirty Nine

The war of Gog-Magog is a much debated issue. Some of the major questions are, is Gog the Antichrist, is this war Armageddon? If not, then who is Gog and when does this war take place?

"The word of the Lord came to me; Son of man, set your face against ***Gog, the land of Magog, the chief prince of Meshech and Tubal;*** *prophesy against him and say: 'This is what the Sovereign Lord says: I am against you, O* ***Gog, chief prince of Meshech and Tubal.*** *I will turn you around, put hooks in your jaws and bring you out with your whole army - your horsemen fully armed, and a great horde with large and small shields, all of them brandishing their swords.* ***Persia, Cush and Put will be with them,*** *all with shields and helmets, also* ***Gomer*** *with all its troops, and* ***Beth Togarmah*** *from the* ***far north*** *with all its troops - the* ***many nations with you.*** *"*
— *Ezekiel 38:1-6*

Questions: Who is Gog? Where is the land of Magog? Where are Meshech, Tubal, Gomer and Beth Togarmah? These are the sons of Noah's son Japheth.

"The sons of Japheth; ***Gomer,*** *and* ***Magog,*** *and Madai, and Javan, and* ***Tubal,*** *and* ***Meshech,*** *and Tiras."* — *Genesis 10:2*

57

Magog, according to Strong H403, is in the mountainous region between Cappadocia and Media, modern Armenia. Meshech, according to Strong H4902, is located north of Armenia towards Iberia. Tubal, according to Strong H8422, located near Cappadocia and associated with Meshech. Gomer, according to Strong H1586, is in the region of Cappadocia and Armenia.

On the above map of the Near East as nations existed just prior to the Babylonian Invasion of Judah, the regions of Media and Cappadocia are circled in grey. Between them, as Strong's states is the region of Magog, the black circle. Today this is Eastern Turkey. Gog from Magog will be a leader of Turkey.

In Ezekiel chapter 27:13 we read "Javan, Tubal, and Meshech, they were thy merchants: they traded the persons of men and vessels of brass in thy market." Ezekiel 27:2 gives the context of Tyre (Lebanon) as the trading markets. Meshech and Tubal traded with the merchants of Tyre. In that day everything moved slowly by land or sea. It is reasonable for the merchants of Meshech and Tubal in the area of eastern Asia Minor to trade with Tyre, as Tyre was a prosperous seaport with access to southern Europe.

However, it is inconceivable that Meshech and Tubal would trade with Tyre if Meshech and Tubal are cities in Russia as some uninformed prophecy teachers proclaim. They would be geographically unsuitable for such trade. They would need to travel through Russia, cross the Caucus Mountain range and then travel across Asia Minor and Syria to get to Tyre. The distance and obstacles are absolutely prohibitive. Besides, why wouldn't they just trade at ports on the Black Sea and load the cargo on sailing ships?

*"And the sons of **Gomer**; Ashkenaz, and Riphath, and **Togarmah**."* — *Genesis 10:3*

Togarmah, according to Strong H8425, is also located in the area of Armenia. Magog, Meshech, Tubal, Gomer and Togarmah are all descendants of Japheth, Noah's son, and settled the region of central and eastern Asia Minor (Turkey). This is also the northern region of the ancient Assyrian Empire. The other nations mentioned:

1. Persia – Iran, Afghanistan, Pakistan
2. Cush – Sudan
3. Put (Phut) – Libya

The major players in the Gog Alliance are Turkey, Iran, Afghanistan, Pakistan, Sudan and Libya. The text also says and "many nations with you."

The "Rosh" issue. Is Russia part of this Alliance? The phrase that some use to include Russia is found in verse 2; "chief prince of Meshech and Tubal." Many popular TV Prophecy teachers translate the phrase "chief prince" as "prince of Rosh."

Rosh, Strong H7218, means head, top, or chief. Rosh is used over 300 times in the Bible and never translated as a proper name. Even if one could force the translation as a proper name, you still cannot link the early Hebrew "rosh" with the early Scandinavian "rus". Thus, Russia is not part of the Gog alliance as a main player. But Russia could be involved under the additional "many nations" phrase.

Who is Gog? He is stated to be the "chief prince of Meshech and Tubal", modern day Turkey. Gog could be a direct reference to Gygez (Gogez, Gugu), a Lydian king who ruled Asia Minor Turkic tribes about 660 B.C. The Scriptures point to Antichrist Gog arising from Turkey as a peacekeeper only to deceive the masses, including the Jews, into a false 7-year peace treaty.

*"Be thou prepared, and prepare for thyself, thou, and all thy company that are assembled unto thee, and be thou a guard unto them. **After many days** thou shalt be visited: in the **latter years** thou shalt come into the land that is brought back from the sword, and is **gathered out of many people, against the mountains of Israel**, which have been always waste: but it is brought forth out of the nations, and they shall dwell safely all of them. Thou shalt ascend and come like a storm, thou shalt be **like a cloud to cover the land**, thou, and all thy bands, and **many people with thee**."* — *Ezekiel 38:7-9*

Antichrist invades Israel as a storm and covers the land as a cloud. In the latter years when Israel is gathered out of many countries back into the land, the Antichrist will come against Israel with many nations and peoples. The prophet Zechariah gives a similar account.

*"Behold, I will make Jerusalem a cup of trembling unto all the people round about, when **they shall be in the siege both against Judah and against Jerusalem**."* — *Zech 12:2*

*"Behold, the day of the LORD cometh, and thy spoil shall be divided in the midst of thee. **For I will gather all nations against Jerusalem to battle; and the city shall be taken, and the houses rifled, and the women ravished; and half of the city shall go forth into captivity,***

and the residue of the people shall not be cut off from the city." —
Zech 14:1-2

The armies of the Antichrist will overrun Israel.

*"Thus saith the Lord GOD; It shall also come to pass, that at the same time shall things come into thy mind, and thou shalt think an evil thought: And thou shalt say, I will go up to the land of unwalled villages; I will go to them that are at rest, that dwell safely, all of them dwelling without walls, and having neither bars nor gates, **To take a spoil, and to take a prey**; to turn thine hand upon the desolate places that are now inhabited, and upon the **people that are gathered out of the nations**, which have gotten cattle and goods, that dwell in the midst of the land. **Sheba, and Dedan, and the merchants of Tarshish**, with all the young lions thereof, shall say unto thee, **Art thou come to take a spoil**? hast thou gathered thy company to take a prey? to carry away silver and gold, to take away cattle and goods, to take a great spoil?" — Ezekiel 38:10-13*

Antichrist invades to take a spoil, to seize great wealth. Sheba and Dedan are modern Saudi Arabia. Tarshish was a city on the Mediterranean in Spain. In a larger context it could refer to Europe. In this case the young lions could be the colonies of Europe all questioning the invasion of Israel for spoil.

*"Therefore, son of man, prophesy and say unto Gog, Thus saith the Lord GOD; In that day when **my people of Israel** dwelleth safely, shalt thou not know it? And thou shalt come from thy place out of the **north parts**, thou, and **many people with thee**, all of them riding upon horses, a great company, and a mighty army: And thou shalt come up against my people of Israel, as **a cloud to cover the land**; it shall be in the **latter days**, and I will bring thee against my land, **that the heathen may know me**, when I shall be sanctified in thee, O Gog,*

before their eyes. Thus saith the Lord GOD; **Art thou he of whom I have spoken in old time** *by my servants the prophets of Israel, which prophesied in those days many years that I would bring thee against them?" — Ezekiel 38:14-17*

God is made known to the heathen thru the demise of Gog. Gog is spoken of by the prophets of old – Isaiah and others. If Gog is not the Antichrist, then whereof was he spoken?

"And it shall come to pass at the **same time when Gog shall come against the land of Israel**, *saith the Lord GOD, that* **my fury shall come up in my face**. *For in my jealousy and in the* **fire of my wrath** *have I spoken, Surely in that day there shall be a* **great shaking in the land of Israel**; *So that the fishes of the sea, and the fowls of the heaven, and the beasts of the field, and all creeping things that creep upon the earth, and all the men that are upon the face of the earth,* **shall shake at my presence**, *and the mountains shall be thrown down, and the steep places shall fall, and every wall shall fall to the ground. And I will call for a sword against him throughout all my mountains, saith the Lord GOD: every man's sword shall be against his brother. And I will plead against him with* **pestilence and with blood**; *and I will rain upon him, and upon his bands, and upon the many people that are with him, an overflowing rain, and* **great hailstones, fire, and brimstone**. *Thus will* **I magnify myself, and sanctify myself; and I will be known in the eyes of many nations, and they shall know that I am the LORD."** *— Ezekiel 38:18-23*

The Lord Jesus is present (shake at my presence) in Israel. He brings an earthquake, pestilence, blood, sword, great hailstones, fire, and brimstone against Gog. Gog will be destroyed; God is magnified and all the heathen shall know that the God of Abraham Isaac and Jacob is the LORD.

Ezekiel 39 highlights:

*"And I will turn thee back, and **leave but the sixth part of thee**, and will cause thee to come up from **the north parts**, and will bring thee upon **the mountains of Israel**: And I will **smite thy bow out of thy left hand**, and will cause thine arrows to fall out of thy right hand. **Thou shalt fall upon the mountains of Israel**, thou, and all thy bands, and the people that is with thee: I will give thee unto the ravenous birds of every sort, and to the beasts of the field to be devoured. Thou shalt fall upon the open field: for I have spoken it, saith the Lord GOD. And I will **send a fire on Magog**, and among them that **dwell carelessly in the isles**: and they shall know that **I am the LORD**."* — *Ezekiel 39:1-6*

5/6th of Gog's armies will be destroyed on the mountains of Israel and their carcasses fed to the wild animals. The rider on the white horse in Rev. 6 is given a bow and sent to conquer. Here we see the bow smitten out of his hand signifying that Gog's days of conquering are finished.

*"So will I make my holy name known in the midst of my people Israel; and **I will not let them pollute my holy name any more: and the heathen shall know that I am the LORD, the Holy One in Israel**. Behold, it is come, and it is done, saith the Lord GOD; **this is the day whereof I have spoken**."* — *Ezekiel 39:7-8*

Holy One IN Israel – Jesus is present in Israel. His name will no longer be blasphemed. Therefore, this war must occur at the end of the tribulation because one of the major traits of the Antichrist is blasphemy of the Lord.

"And they that dwell in the cities of Israel shall go forth, and shall set on fire and burn the weapons, both the shields and the bucklers, the bows and the arrows, and the handstaves, and the spears, and they

*shall burn them with fire seven years: So that they shall take no wood out of the field, neither cut down any out of the forests; for they shall burn the weapons with fire: and they shall spoil those that spoiled them, and rob those that robbed them, saith the Lord GOD. And it shall come to pass in that day, that I will give unto Gog a place there of graves in Israel, the valley of the passengers on the east of the sea: and it shall stop the noses of the passengers: and there shall they **bury Gog and all his multitude**: and they shall call it The valley of Hamongog. And seven months shall the house of Israel be burying of them, that they may cleanse the land. Yea, all the people of the land shall bury them; and it shall be to them a renown the **day that I shall be glorified, saith the Lord GOD**.*" — *Ezekiel 39:9-13*

Gog and his armies are buried in Israel.

*"And they shall **sever out men of continual employment**, passing through the land to bury with the passengers those that remain upon the face of the earth, to cleanse it: after the end of seven months shall they search. And the passengers that pass through the land, when any seeth a man's bone, then shall he set up a sign by it, till the buriers have buried it in the valley of Hamongog. And also the name of the city shall be Hamonah. Thus **shall they cleanse the land**.*" — *Ezekiel 39:14-16*

A mass graveyard has been set up east of the Dead Sea and teams of men search the land of Israel to cleanse the land of any human remains. This sounds like a first century description of HAZMAT teams searching for contaminated remains.

*"And, thou son of man, thus saith the Lord GOD; Speak unto every **feathered fowl**, and to every **beast of the field**, Assemble yourselves, and come; gather yourselves on every side to **my sacrifice** that I do sacrifice for you, even a **great sacrifice upon the mountains of Israel**,*

64

*that ye may eat flesh, and drink blood. Ye shall eat the flesh of the mighty, and drink the blood of the princes of the earth, of rams, of lambs, and of goats, of bullocks, all of them **fatlings of Bashan**. And ye shall eat fat till ye be full, and drink blood till ye be drunken, of my sacrifice which I have sacrificed for you. Thus ye shall be filled at my table with horses and chariots, with mighty men, and with all men of war, saith the Lord GOD."* — *Ezekiel 39:17-20*

Fatlings of Bashan – Syrians; a great slaughter of Syrians at Bashan, Syria.

*"And I will set my glory among the heathen, and all the **heathen shall see my judgment** that I have executed, and **my hand that I have laid upon them**. So the house of Israel shall know that I am the LORD their God from that day and forward. And the heathen shall know that the house of Israel went into captivity for their iniquity: because they trespassed against me, therefore **hid I my face from them**, and gave them into the hand of their enemies: so fell they all by the sword. According to their uncleanness and according to their transgressions have I done unto them, and **hid my face from them**."* — *Ezekiel 39:21-24*

Israel was sent into captivity by the Lord for their iniquity. He has hidden His face from them for two thousand years. There is still another captivity in the future but from that day forward they will know that Jesus is their Lord.

*"Come, and let us return unto the LORD: for he hath torn, and he will heal us; he hath smitten, and he will bind us up. After **two days will he revive us**: in the **third day he will raise us up**, and we shall live in his sight."* — *Hosea 6:1-2*

65

For a day is as a thousand years with the Lord. The third day is the Millennial Reign of the Lord Jesus.

*"Therefore thus saith the Lord GOD; Now will I bring again the captivity of Jacob, and have mercy upon the whole house of Israel, and will be jealous for my holy name; After that they have borne their shame, and all their trespasses whereby they have trespassed against me, when they dwelt safely in their land, and none made them afraid. When I have brought them again from the people, and gathered them out of their enemies' lands, and am sanctified in them in the sight of many nations; Then shall they know that I am the LORD their God, which caused them to be led into captivity among the heathen: but **I have gathered them unto their own land**, and have left none of them anymore there. **Neither will I hide my face any more from them**: for I have poured out my spirit upon the house of Israel, saith the Lord GOD." — Ezekiel 39:25-29*

Summary of Ezekiel 38 & 39:
- o Gog is a ruler that leads a group of Middle Eastern nations in a war against Israel.
- o The nations include Turkey, Iran, Afghanistan, Pakistan, Sudan and Libya and many others including Syria.
- o The war takes place in the latter days when Israel is secure.
- o Gog invades to take a spoil and prey.
- o Arabia and possibly Europe will protest.
- o Gog is spoken of by the prophets of old.
- o God's fury will be in His face over the invasion.
- o All will shake at the presence of God.
- o God will fight with the sword, pestilence, rain, great hailstones, fire, and brimstone.
- o Gog will die on the mountains of Israel.
- o God will send fire on Magog (possibly Turkey, Syria, or Iran)

- o God's name will no longer be blasphemed.
- o Burn weapons for seven years.
- o Bury bodies for seven months.
- o Mass graveyard east of the Dead Sea
- o God prepares a great sacrifice of Syrians for the birds and wild beasts.
- o God's Holy Name sanctified.
- o God's Spirit poured out upon the house of Israel.

Gog is the Antichrist, and this war is Armageddon.

The traditional view is the Gog war and Armageddon are two different battles. However, Jewish rabbis and sages throughout history have stated that Gog and Magog are indeed the final evil world ruler and his armies that will attack Israel and be defeated by the Messiah.

One argument claims the Gog war involves a limited number of nations, but Armageddon encompasses the entire world. In fact, both the Gog and Armageddon wars involve a limited number of nations. The Gog Coalition is limited to Middle Eastern nations. Joining Turkey and Iran are:

*"...**Persia, Ethiopia**, and **Libya** are with them... **Gomer** and all its troops; the house of **Togarmah** from the far north and all its troops—many people are with you.... In the latter years... You will ascend, coming like a storm, covering the land like a cloud, you and all your troops and many peoples with you."* — Ezekiel 38:1-9

The Antichrist's Empire is primarily a Ten Nation Group. Ten Toes & Horns of Daniel 2, Daniel 7, Revelation 13, 17

*"And the ten horns which thou sawest are **ten kings**, which have received no kingdom as yet; but **receive power as kings one hour with the beast.** "* — Revelation 17:12

The Antichrist's rule will not be global. The primary verse used to conclude a global rule of the Antichrist:

"He (the Antichrist) was given power to make war against the saints and to conquer them. And he was given authority over every tribe, people, language and nation. **ALL** *inhabitants of the* **earth** *will worship the beast —* **ALL** *whose names have not been written in the book of life belonging to the Lamb that was slain from the creation of the world." — Revelation 13:7-8*

Earth means the land, in this case the whole land of the Middle East. Strong's G1093 is *"ge"*, the Greek word for earth in the above verse. It means arable land, the ground, the mainland, the inhabited earth, a country, land enclosed with fixed boundaries, territory of region. The word earth is restricted to a particular land, in this case the land of the Middle East.

In contrast to the Greek word "ge" is the word "cosmos" that means the entire world, the universe, the circle of the earth. The difference is easily distinguishable.

"The **kingdoms of this world** *(cosmos) are become the* **kingdoms of our Lord, and of his Christ**; *and he shall* **reign for ever and ever**.*"* — *Revelation 11:15*

The Antichrist will rule over the land (earth) of the Middle East, but the Lord Jesus Christ will rule the cosmos. Be careful not to interpret hyperbole too literally! All will not worship the Antichrist. "ALL whose names have not been written in the book of life" will worship the Antichrist.

Not only will there be individuals resisting the Antichrist's rule, but nations will resist the Antichrist also. The judgment of the nation proves there are good and evil nations.

"When the Son of man shall come in his glory, and all the holy angels with him, then shall he sit upon the throne of his glory: And before

him **shall be gathered all nations**: *and he shall separate them one from another, as a shepherd divideth his* **sheep** *from the* **goats**: *And he shall set the sheep on his right hand, but the goats on the left. Then shall the King say unto them on his right hand, Come, ye blessed of my Father, inherit the kingdom prepared for you from the foundation of the world. . . Verily I say unto you, Inasmuch as ye have done it unto one of the least of these my brethren, ye have done it unto me."*
— *Matthew 25: 31-40*

The sheep nations are those that resisted the Antichrist's rule and helped Israel. We know that the Antichrist Coalition does not include every nation on the earth because the Bible clearly states that some nations will resist the Antichrist and even fight against him.

"For I will gather **ALL nations against Jerusalem to battle***; and the city shall be taken, and the houses rifled, and the women ravished; and half of the city shall go forth into captivity"* — *Zechariah 14:2*

Who are "ALL nations"?

"I am going to make Jerusalem a cup that sends **all the surrounding peoples reeling***. Judah will be besieged as well as Jerusalem."* — *Zechariah 12:2*

"Judah also will fight at Jerusalem; and the wealth of **all the surrounding nations** *will be gathered, gold and silver and garments in great abundance."* — *Zechariah 14:14*

"Hasten and come, **all you surrounding nations***, And gather yourselves there. Bring down, O LORD, Your mighty ones. Let the nations be aroused and come up to the valley of Jehoshaphat, For there I will sit to judge* **All the surrounding nations***."*
—*Joel 3:11-12*

*"No longer will the people of Israel **have malicious neighbors** who are painful briers and sharp thorns. Then they will know that I am the Sovereign LORD. They will live in safety when **I inflict punishment on all their neighbors** who maligned them. Then they will know that I am the LORD their God."* — Ezekiel 28:24-26

Remember: While Jesus is portrayed throughout the Old Testament as engaging in battle and judging Middle Eastern Nations, never once in the entire Bible is any European nation ever mentioned in this context. Only Middle Eastern nations are judged.

Another supposed contrast between Gog and Armageddon is the purpose of the Gog invasion is to take spoil and the purpose of the Armageddon Campaign is to destroy all the Jews and prevent the second coming of Jesus Christ.

Gog Invasion:

*"On that day... you will make an evil plan: You will say, 'I will go up against a land of unwalled villages... **to take plunder and to take booty**, to stretch out your hand against the waste places that are again inhabited, and against a people gathered from the nations, who have acquired livestock and goods, who dwell in the midst of the land."* — Ezekiel 38:10-13

Armageddon:

*"Behold, the day of the Lord cometh, and thy **spoil shall be divided in the midst of thee**. For I will gather all nations against Jerusalem to battle; and the city shall be taken... "*
— Zechariah 14:1-2

"Woe to the Assyrian (the Antichrist), the rod of my anger, in whose hand is the club of my wrath... I dispatch him against a people who

anger me, **to seize loot and snatch plunder,** *and to trample them down like mud in the streets."* — *Isaiah 10:5-7*

"When the richest provinces feel secure, he will invade them... **He will distribute plunder, loot, and wealth among his followers."** — *Daniel 11:24*

Zechariah, Isaiah, and Daniel speak of the Armageddon war at the second coming of Christ. Both the Gog war and Armageddon are to take a spoil.

"In the last-days of the Islamic community, the Mahdi will appear... **He will give away wealth profusely,** flocks will be in abundance, and the Muslim community will be large and honored..." — Sahih Hakim Mustadrak.

"In those years my community will enjoy a time of happiness such as they have never experienced before. ... A man will stand and say, **"Give to me Mahdi!" and he will say, "Take."** — At-Tabarani

Even the Muslims know that the end time ruler will plunder and loot in keeping with their prophet Muhammad.

Lastly, some argue that the Ezekiel invasion comes from the North, but the Armageddon invasion comes from the whole Earth proving they are different wars.

Gog Invasion:

"In that day, when my people Israel are living in safety, will you not take notice of it? You will come from **your place in the far north,** *you and many nations with you... a mighty army... You will advance against my people Israel like a cloud that covers the land... I am*

*against you, O Gog... I will **bring you from the far north** and send you against the mountains of Israel." — Ezekiel 38:14-16; 39:1-3*

Armageddon:

*"I will drive the **northern army** far from you, pushing it into a parched and barren land, with its front columns going into the eastern sea and those in the rear into the western sea. And its stench will go up; its smell will rise." — Joel 2:20*

*"Then the LORD said unto me, **Out of the north an evil shall break forth** upon all the inhabitants of the land." — Jeremiah 1:14*

*"Set up the standard toward Zion: retire, stay not: for **I will bring evil from the north**, and a great destruction." — Jeremiah 4:6*

*"For this is the day of the Lord GOD of hosts, a day of vengeance, that he may avenge him of his adversaries: and the sword shall devour, and it shall be satiate and made drunk with their blood: for the Lord GOD of hosts **hath a sacrifice in the north country by the river Euphrates**." — Jeremiah 46:10*

      Concluding thoughts regarding these major arguments that Gog and the Antichrist are two different persons: Gog and the Antichrist are in fact the same person both coming from the north and the war of Gog and Armageddon are the same campaign occurring in the same region. Comparison of Ezekiel 38 & 39 with Revelation and other Day of the Lord verses show that the war of Magog is just another view of Armageddon.

      This list is certainly not exhaustive; many verses proclaim the Day of the Lord in the Old and New Testaments. Again, many thanks to Walid Shoebat and his book "God's War on Terror" for the inspiration for the chart below.

Ezekiel 38-39 – Gog War	Armageddon
"Gog shall come against the land of Israel" 38:18	"And he gathered them together into a place called in the Hebrew tongue Armageddon." Rev 16:16
"Surely in that day there shall be a great shaking in the land of Israel;" 38:19	"and there was a great earthquake, such as was not since men were upon the earth, so mighty an earthquake, and so great." Rev 16:18
"and the mountains shall be thrown down" 38:20	"And every island fled away, and the mountains were not found." Rev 16:20
"and the steep places shall fall, and every wall shall fall to the ground." 38:20	"And the great city was divided into three parts, and the cities of the nation's fell" Rev 16:19
"an overflowing rain, and great hailstones, fire, and brimstone" 38:22	"And there fell upon men a great hail out of heaven, every stone about the weight of a talent:" Rev 16:21
"And I will plead against him with pestilence and with blood;" 38:22	"And this shall be the plague wherewith the LORD will smite all the people that have fought against Jerusalem; Their flesh shall consume away while they stand upon their feet, and their eyes shall consume away in their holes, and their tongue shall consume away in their mouth." Zech 14:12
"And ye shall eat fat till ye be full, and drink blood till ye be drunken, of my sacrifice which I have sacrificed for you."	"Hold thy peace at the presence of the Lord GOD: for the day of the LORD is at hand: for the LORD hath prepared a

39:19	sacrifice, he hath bid his guests." Zeph 1:7
"And, thou son of man, thus saith the Lord GOD; Speak unto every feathered fowl, and to every beast of the field, Assemble yourselves, and come; gather yourselves on every side to my sacrifice that I do sacrifice for you, even a great sacrifice upon the mountains of Israel, that ye may eat flesh, and drink blood. Ye shall eat the flesh of the mighty, and drink the blood of the princes of the earth, of rams, of lambs, and of goats, of bullocks, all of them fatlings of Bashan. And ye shall eat fat till ye be full, and drink blood till ye be drunken, of my sacrifice which I have sacrificed for you." 39:17-19	"And I saw an angel standing in the sun; and he cried with a loud voice, saying to all the fowls that fly in the midst of heaven, Come and gather yourselves together unto the supper of the great God; That ye may eat the flesh of kings, and the flesh of captains, and the flesh of mighty men, and the flesh of horses, and of them that sit on them, and the flesh of all men, both free and bond, both small and great." Rev 19:17-18
"And I will call for a sword against him throughout all my mountains, saith the Lord GOD: every man's sword shall be against his brother." 38:21	"And it shall come to pass in that day, that a great tumult from the LORD shall be among them; and they shall lay hold everyone on the hand of his neighbour, and his hand shall rise up against the hand of his neighbour." Zech 14:13
"Persia, Ethiopia, and Libya with them; all of them with shield and helmet:" 38:5	"and the Libyans and the Ethiopians shall be at his steps." Dan 11:43
"and the heathen shall know that I am the LORD, the	"And I saw heaven opened, and behold a white horse; and he

Holy One in Israel." 39:7	that sat upon him was called Faithful and True, and in righteousness he doth judge and make war." Rev 19:11 "Then shall the LORD go forth, and fight against those nations, as when he fought in the day of battle." Zech 14:3
"So will I make my holy name known in the midst of my people Israel; and I will not let them pollute my holy name any more:" 39:7	"But this shall be the covenant that I will make with the house of Israel; After those days, saith the LORD, I will put my law in their inward parts, and write it in their hearts; and will be their God, and they shall be my people." Jer 31:33
"Behold, it is come, and it is done, saith the Lord GOD; this is the day whereof I have spoken." 39:8	"And the seventh angel poured out his vial into the air; and there came a great voice out of the temple of heaven, from the throne, saying, It is done." Rev 16:17
"will cause thee to come up from the north parts, and will bring thee upon the mountains of Israel:" 39:2	"But I will remove far off from you the northern army, and will drive him into a land barren and desolate" Joel 2:20
"To take a spoil, and to take a prey;" 38:12	"Behold, the day of the LORD cometh, and thy spoil shall be divided in the midst of thee." Zech 14:1

Part Five

Judgment of Islamic Nations

Chapter Eleven

The Gathered Nations

*"I will also **gather all nations**, and will bring them down into the valley of Jehoshaphat, and will plead with them there for my people and for my heritage Israel, whom they have scattered among the **nations**, and parted my land."* — *Joel 3:2*

*"Therefore wait ye upon me, saith the LORD, until the day that I rise up to the prey: for my determination is to **gather the nations**, that I may assemble the kingdoms, to pour upon them mine indignation, even all my fierce anger: for all the earth shall be devoured with the fire of my jealousy."* — *Zephaniah 3:8*

*"And it shall come to pass in that day, that I will seek to destroy **all the nations that come against Jerusalem**."* — *Zechariah 12:9*

*"For I will **gather all nations** against Jerusalem to battle; and the city shall be taken, and the houses rifled, and the women ravished; and half of the city shall go forth into captivity, and the residue of the people shall not be cut off from the city. Then shall the LORD go*

*forth, and fight against those **nations**, as when he fought in the day of battle."* — *Zechariah 14:2-3*

*"And out of his mouth goeth a sharp sword, that with it he should **smite the nations**: and he shall rule them with a rod of iron: and he treadeth the winepress of the fierceness and wrath of Almighty God."* — *Revelation 19:15*

The Lord Jesus Christ will gather, judge and make war with the nations.

But just who are the nations from a Biblical perspective? The word *"nations" - Strong H1471 – a people;* Genesis chapter ten gives a description of the Biblical nations that descended from Noah.

*"Now these are the generations of the **sons of Noah, Shem, Ham, and Japheth**: and unto them were sons born after the flood. The **sons of Japheth**; Gomer, and Magog, and Madai, and Javan, and Tubal, and Meshech, and Tiras. And the sons of Gomer; Ashkenaz, and Riphath, and Togarmah. And the sons of Javan; Elishah, and Tarshish, Kittim, and Dodanim. By these were the isles of the Gentiles divided in their lands; every one after his tongue, after their families, **in their nations**."* — *Genesis 10:1-5*

*"And the **sons of Ham**; Cush, and Mizraim, and Phut, and Canaan. And the sons of Cush; Seba, and Havilah, and Sabtah, and Raamah, and Sabtecha: and the sons of Raamah; Sheba, and Dedan. And Cush begat **Nimrod**: he began to be a mighty one in the earth. He was a mighty hunter before the LORD: wherefore it is said, Even as Nimrod the mighty hunter before the LORD. And the beginning of his kingdom was*

Babel, and Erech, and Accad, and Calneh, in the **land of Shinar**. *Out of that land went forth **Asshur**, and builded **Nineveh**...*" — *Genesis 10:6-11*

*"These are the sons of Ham, after their families, after their tongues, in their countries, **and in their nations**."* — *Genesis 10:20*

*"Unto **Shem** also, the father of all the children of Eber, the brother of Japheth the elder, even to him were children born. The children of Shem; Elam, and Asshur, and Arphaxad, and Lud, and Aram. And the children of Aram; Uz, and Hul, and Gether, and Mash... These are the sons of Shem, after their families, after their tongues, in their lands, **after their nations**."* — *Genesis 10:21-31*

"These are the families of the sons of Noah, after their generations, in their nations: and by these were the nations divided in the earth after the flood." — *Genesis 10:32*

The Biblical Nations are the nations of the greater Middle East and Asia Minor. These are the very nations that the Lord will judge upon His return.

Edom – the generations of Esau – Genesis 36:1.

*"Come near, **ye nations**, to hear; and hearken, ye people: let the earth hear, and all that is therein; the world, and all things that come forth of it. **For the indignation of the LORD is upon all nations**, and his fury upon all their armies: he hath utterly destroyed them, he hath delivered them to the **slaughter**. Their slain also shall be cast out, and their stink shall come up out of their carcases, and the mountains shall be melted with their blood. And all the host of heaven shall be dissolved, and the heavens shall be rolled together as a scroll: and all*

their host shall fall down, as the leaf falleth off from the vine, and as a falling fig from the fig tree. **For my sword shall be bathed in heaven: behold, it shall come down upon Idumea, and upon the people of my curse, to judgment.** *The sword of the LORD is filled with blood, it is made fat with fatness, and with the blood of lambs and goats, with the fat of the kidneys of rams: for the* **LORD hath a sacrifice in Bozrah, and a great slaughter in the land of Idumea.** *And the unicorns shall come down with them, and the bullocks with the bulls; and their* **land shall be soaked with blood,** *and their dust made fat with fatness.* **For it is the day of the LORD'S vengeance, and the year of recompences for the controversy of Zion.** *And the streams thereof shall be* **turned into pitch,** *and the dust thereof into* **brimstone,** *and the land thereof shall become* **burning pitch.** *It shall not be quenched night nor day; the* **smoke thereof shall go up forever:** *from generation to generation it shall lie waste; none shall pass through it for ever and ever." — Isaiah 34:1-10*

Greater Edom (Idumea, Bozrah) includes western and southern Arabia. The vengeance of the Lord is upon them for the controversy of Zion. Jordan and Arabia will be destroyed, and the oil fields will be turned into burning pitch.

*"**Concerning Edom,** thus saith the LORD of hosts; Is wisdom no more in Teman? is counsel perished from the prudent? is their wisdom vanished? Flee ye, turn back, dwell deep,* **O inhabitants of Dedan;** *… For thus saith the LORD; Behold, they whose judgment was not to drink of the cup have assuredly drunken; and art thou he that shall altogether go unpunished? thou shalt not go unpunished, but thou shalt surely drink of it. For I have sworn by myself, saith the LORD, that* **Bozrah shall become a desolation, a reproach, a waste, and a curse; and all the cities thereof shall be perpetual wastes.** *I have heard a rumour from the LORD, and an ambassador is sent unto the*

*heathen, saying, Gather ye together, and come against her, and rise up to the battle. For, lo, I will make thee small among the heathen, and despised among men. Thy terribleness hath deceived thee, and the pride of thine heart, O thou that dwellest in the clefts of the rock, that holdest the height of the hill: though thou shouldest make thy nest as high as the eagle, I will bring thee down from thence, saith the LORD. **Also Edom shall be a desolation***: every one that goeth by it shall be astonished, and shall hiss at all the plagues thereof. As in the overthrow of Sodom and Gomorrah and the neighbour cities thereof, saith the LORD, no man shall abide there, neither shall a son of man dwell in it. Behold, he shall come up like a lion from the swelling of Jordan against the habitation of the strong: but I will suddenly make him run away from her: and who is a chosen man, that I may appoint over her? for who is like me? and who will appoint me the time? and who is that shepherd that will stand before me? Therefore hear the* **counsel of the LORD, that he hath taken against Edom**; *and his purposes, that he hath purposed against the inhabitants of* **Teman**: *Surely the least of the flock shall draw them out: surely he shall make their habitations desolate with them. The **earth is moved at the noise of their fall, at the cry the noise thereof was heard in the Red sea.** Behold, he shall come up and fly as the eagle, and spread his wings over* **Bozrah**: *and at* **that day shall the heart of the mighty men of Edom be as the heart of a woman in her pangs**." —*Jeremiah 49:7-22*

Greater Edom, Dedan (Arabia), Bozrah, Teman will be destroyed with a great noise that is heard in the Red Sea. This happens in "that day", the Day of the Lord. What great city of Islam is located in Arabia near the Red Sea? Mecca.

*"There is **Edom**, her kings, and all her princes, which with their might are laid by them that were **slain by the sword**: they shall lie*

81

with the uncircumcised, and with them that go down to the pit." — *Ezekiel 32:29*

*"**Who is this that cometh from Edom, with dyed garments from Bozrah?** this that is glorious in his apparel, travelling in the greatness of his strength? I that speak in righteousness, mighty to save. **Wherefore art thou red in thine apparel**, and thy garments like him that treadeth in the winefat? I have trodden the winepress alone; and of the people there was none with me: for **I will tread them in mine anger, and trample them in my fury; and their blood shall be sprinkled upon my garments, and I will stain all my raiment**. For the day of **vengeance is in mine heart**, and the year of my redeemed is come. And I looked, and there was none to help; and I wondered that there was none to uphold: therefore mine own arm brought salvation unto me; and my fury, it upheld me. **And I will tread down the people in mine anger, and make them drunk in my fury**, and I will bring down their strength to the earth."* — *Isaiah 63:1-6*

The Lord comes from Edom and Bozrah in anger, fury and vengeance with garments stained with the blood of His enemies. Wow, this is a powerful scene of the Lord's vengeance, unfamiliar to most Christians.

*"Moreover the word of the LORD came unto me, saying, Son of man, **set thy face against mount Seir, and prophesy against it**, And say unto it, Thus saith the Lord GOD; Behold, O mount Seir, I am against thee, and I will stretch out mine hand against thee, and **I will make thee most desolate**. I will lay thy cities waste, and thou shalt be desolate, and thou shalt know that I am the LORD... As thou didst rejoice at the inheritance of the house of Israel, because it was desolate, so will I do unto thee: **thou shalt be desolate, O mount Seir, and all***

Idumea, *even all of it: and they shall know that I am the LORD."*
— Ezekiel 35:1–4, 15

The Burden of Egypt.

*"**The burden of Egypt. Behold, the LORD rideth upon a swift cloud, and shall come into Egypt:** and the idols of Egypt shall be moved **at his presence**, and the heart of Egypt shall melt in the midst of it. And I will set the Egyptians against the Egyptians: and they shall fight every one against his brother, and every one against his neighbour; city against city, and kingdom against kingdom. And the **spirit of Egypt shall fail** in the midst thereof; and I will destroy the counsel thereof: and they shall seek to the idols, and to the charmers, and to them that have familiar spirits, and to the wizards. And the Egyptians will I give over into the hand of a cruel lord; and a fierce king shall rule over them, saith the Lord, the LORD of hosts... **In that day shall Egypt be like unto women: and it shall be afraid and fear because of the shaking of the hand of the LORD of hosts**, which he shaketh over it..."* — Isaiah 19:1–16

The Burden of Moab (Jordan).

*"**The burden of Moab**. Because in the night Ar of Moab is **laid waste**, and brought to silence; because in the night Kir of Moab is **laid waste**, and brought to silence; He is gone up to Bajith, and to Dibon, the high places, to weep: Moab shall howl over Nebo, and over Medeba: on all their heads shall be baldness, and every beard cut off. In their streets they shall gird themselves with sackcloth: on the tops of their houses, and in their streets, every one shall howl, weeping abundantly. And Heshbon shall cry, and Elealeh: their voice shall be heard even unto Jahaz: therefore the armed soldiers of Moab shall cry out; his life shall be grievous unto him."* — Isaiah 15:1–3

*"And it shall be said in **that day**, Lo, this is our God; we have waited for him, and he will save us: this is the LORD; we have waited for him, we will be glad and rejoice in his salvation. For in this mountain shall the hand of the LORD rest, and **Moab shall be trodden down under him, even as straw is trodden down for the dunghill**."* — Isaiah 25:9-10

The Burden of Damascus.

*"The burden of Damascus. Behold, **Damascus is taken away from being a city**, and it shall be a **ruinous heap**."* — Isaiah 17:1

The Burden of Tyre.

*The **burden of Tyre**. Howl, ye ships of Tarshish; for it is **laid waste**,* — Isaiah 23:1

Who are the nations that drink the wine cup of the Lord's wrath?

*"For thus saith the LORD God of Israel unto me; **Take the wine cup of this fury at my hand, and cause all the nations, to whom I send thee, to drink it.** And they shall drink, and be moved, and be mad, because of the sword that I will send among them. Then took I the cup at the LORD'S hand, and made all the nations to drink, unto whom the LORD had sent me: To wit, **Jerusalem, and the cities of Judah,** and the kings thereof, and the princes thereof, to make them a desolation, an astonishment, an hissing, and a curse; as it is this day; **Pharaoh king of Egypt**, and his servants, and his princes, and all his people; And all the **mingled people**, and all the kings of the land of Uz, and all the kings of the land of **the Philistines**, and Ashkelon, and Azzah, and Ekron, and the remnant of Ashdod, **Edom, and Moab, and the children of Ammon,** And all the **kings of Tyrus**, and*

*all the **kings of Zidon**, and the kings of the isles which are beyond the sea, **Dedan, and Tema**, and Buz, and all that are in the utmost corners, And all the **kings of Arabia**, and all the kings of the **mingled people that dwell in the desert**, And all the kings of Zimri, and all the kings of **Elam**, and all the kings of the **Medes**, And all the **kings of the north**, far and near, one with another, and all the kingdoms of the world, which are upon the face of the earth: and the king of Sheshach shall drink after them. Therefore thou shalt say unto them, Thus saith the LORD of hosts, the God of Israel; **Drink ye, and be drunken**, and spue, and fall, and rise no more, because of **the sword which I will send among you**. And it shall be, if they refuse to take the cup at thine hand to drink, then shalt thou say unto them, Thus saith the LORD of hosts; Ye shall certainly drink. For, lo, I begin to bring evil on the city which is called by my name, and should ye be utterly unpunished? Ye shall not be unpunished: **for I will call for a sword upon all the inhabitants of the earth**, saith the LORD of hosts. Therefore prophesy thou against them all these words, and say unto them, The LORD shall roar from on high, and utter his voice from his holy habitation; he shall mightily roar upon his habitation; he shall give a shout, as they that tread the grapes, against all the inhabitants of the earth. A noise shall come even to the ends of the earth; **for the LORD hath a controversy with the nations**, he will plead with all flesh; he will give them that are wicked to the sword, saith the LORD. Thus saith the LORD of hosts, Behold, evil shall go forth from nation to nation, and a great whirlwind shall be raised up from the coasts of the earth. And the slain of the LORD shall be at that day from one end of the earth even unto the other end of the earth: they shall not be lamented, neither gathered, nor buried; they shall be dung upon the ground. Howl, ye shepherds, and cry; and wallow yourselves in the ashes, ye principal of the flock: for the days of your slaughter and of your dispersions are accomplished; and ye shall fall like a pleasant vessel. And the shepherds shall have no way to* *flee, nor the principal of the flock to escape. A voice of the cry of the shepherds, and an howling of the principal of the flock, shall be heard: for the LORD hath spoiled their pasture. And the peaceable habitations are cut down because of the fierce anger of the LORD. He hath forsaken his covert, as the lion: for their land is desolate because of the fierceness of the oppressor, and because of his fierce anger."* — *Jeremiah 25:15-38*

"For the day is near, even the **day of the LORD is near**, *a cloudy day; it shall be the* **time of the heathen***. And the* **sword shall come upon Egypt**, *and* **great pain shall be in Ethiopia**, *when the slain shall fall in Egypt, and they shall take away her multitude, and her foundations shall be broken down.* **Ethiopia, and Libya, and Lydia, and all the mingled people***, and Chub, and the men of the land that is in league, shall fall with them by the sword. Thus saith the LORD; They also that uphold Egypt shall fall; and the pride of her power shall come down: from the tower of Syene shall they fall in it by the sword, saith the Lord GOD. And they shall be desolate in the midst of the countries that are desolate, and her cities shall be in the midst of the cities that are wasted. And they shall know that I am the LORD, when I have set a fire in Egypt, and when all her helpers shall be destroyed."* — *Ezekiel 30:3-8*

All of the Nations that the Lord judges upon His return are Middle Easter Muslim nations that surround Israel.

What about the Palestinian people? Are they mentioned in Bible prophecy? No, they are not because the concept of a Palestinian people is a myth created primarily by Jordan and Syria to be used as propaganda against Israel.

Samuel Clemens (Mark Twain) visited the Holy Land in 1867 and recorded the following in his book "The Innocents Abroad" chapter 56. "Of all the lands there are for dismal scenery, I think Palestine must be the prince. The hills are barren, they are dull of color, they are unpicturesque in shape. The valleys are unsightly deserts fringed with a feeble vegetation that has an expression about it of being sorrowful and despondent. The Dead Sea and the Sea of Galilee sleep in the midst of a vast stretch of hill and plain wherein the eye rests upon no pleasant tint, no striking object, no soft picture dreaming in a purple haze or mottled with the shadows of the clouds. Every outline is harsh, every feature is distinct, there is no perspective—distance works no enchantment here. It is a hopeless, dreary, heart-broken land. Palestine is desolate and unlovely. And why should it be otherwise? Can the curse of the Deity beautify a land?" Mr. Clemens portrays quite a desolate picture with no mention of an indigenous Palestinian people.

The Land of Palestine in the mid-19th century was desolate. The so-called Palestinian people actually do not exist as an indigenous people group in the Holy Land of Israel. Well, then who are the so-called Palestinian refugees?

After the Jews started immigrating back to the land of Israel at the end of the 19th Century the land started to blossom and become productive. There was a continuing need for workers in both the prospering agricultural enterprises and the cities. Poor Bedouin Arabs from Jordan and Syria primarily filled the need.

When Israel was attacked in 1948 these Arab workers were told by the attacking nations to leave Israel just before the war. They were anticipating a quick Arab victory and a return to Israel to reap the spoils of war. But the attacking Arab nations lost the war. The nation of Israel actually invited them back to work in Israel, but the Jordanians prevented them from returning and even to this day holds them in refugee camps solely for political purposes.

These refugees could have been easily absorbed back into the populace of Israel, Jordan and Syria but they are now just pawns in the Middle East chess game.

Part Six
Mark of the Beast

Chapter Twelve
The Beasts of Revelation Chapter Thirteen

*"And I stood upon the **sand of the sea**, and saw **a beast rise up out of the sea**, having **seven heads and ten horns**, and upon his horns **ten crowns**, and upon his heads the name of blasphemy. And the beast which I saw was **like unto a leopard**, and his feet were as **the feet of a bear**, and his mouth as the **mouth of a lion**: and the **dragon gave him his power**, and his seat, and **great authority**. And I saw **one of his heads as it were wounded to death**; and his **deadly wound was healed**: and all the world wondered after the beast. And they worshipped the dragon which gave power unto the beast: and they worshipped the beast, saying, Who is like unto the beast? who is able to make war with him? And there was **given unto him a mouth speaking great things and blasphemies**; and power was given unto him to **continue forty and two months**. And he opened his mouth in blasphemy against God, to blaspheme his name, and his tabernacle, and them that dwell in heaven. And it was given unto him to make war with the saints, and to overcome them: and power was given*

*him over **all kindreds, and tongues, and nations**. And all that dwell upon the earth shall worship him, whose names are not written in the book of life of the Lamb slain from the foundation of the world. If any man have an ear, let him hear. He that leadeth into captivity shall go into captivity: he that killeth with the sword must be killed with the sword. Here is the patience and the faith of the saints."* — *Revelation 13:1-10*

The following points define this beast:

- o The above beast is both a PERSON and a KINGDOM that arises from the sea of humanity in the Middle East
- o This kingdom has seven heads and ten horns, similar to the 10 toes of the image in Daniel 2 and the fourth beast of Daniel 7 with 10 horns.
- o This kingdom has the attributes and geological area of the leopard (Grecian kingdom), a bear (Persian kingdom), and the lion (Babylonian kingdom).
- o Satan, the dragon, empowers the kingdom.
- o One of the seven heads is wounded and then healed. These seven heads are prior kingdoms one of which is defeated (wounded) but is revived (healed) during the last days.
- o This kingdom is given a mouth speaking great blasphemies, the Antichrist.
- o The Kingdom and its King (Antichrist) continue 42 months, 3 ½ years.
- o The seven heads are identified in the chapter on revelation 17.

*"And I beheld **another beast coming up out of the earth**; and he had two horns **like a lamb**, and he **spake as a dragon**. ¹²And he exerciseth all the power of the first beast before him, and causeth the earth and them which dwell therein to worship the first beast, whose deadly wound was healed. And he doeth **great wonders**, so that he **maketh***

fire come down from heaven on the earth in the sight of men, And *deceiveth them that dwell on the earth* by the means of those miracles which he had power to do in the sight of the beast; saying to them that dwell on the earth, that they should make an **image to the beast**, which had the wound by a sword, and did live. ⁵*And he had power to give life unto the image of the beast*, that the image of the beast should both speak, and cause that as many as **would not worship the image of the beast should be killed.** And he causeth all, both small and great, rich and poor, free and bond, to receive a mark in their **right hand**, or in their **foreheads**: And that no man might buy or sell, save he that had the **mark, or the name of the beast, or the number of his name.** Here is wisdom. Let him that hath understanding count the **number of the beast**: for it is the number of a man; and his number is **Six hundred threescore and six.**" — *Revelation 13:11-18*

- o This beast that comes from the earth (land) is a man, he is the False Prophet.
- o He is like a lamb, a counterfeit messiah or prophet.
- o He does great signs and wonders that deceive those living on earth whose names are not written in the Lambs book of life.
- o He imitates the Prophet Elijah by calling fire down from heaven. He is a false fulfillment of Malachi 4:5 "Behold, I will send you Elijah the prophet before the coming of the great and dreadful day of the LORD."
- o He creates an image of the first beast kingdom.
- o All must worship the image or suffer death.
- o All must receive a mark in their forehead or right hand (arm) to survive.

The traditional interpretation of Revelation 13 is that the first beast is the Antichrist, and the second beast is the False Prophet. The first beast, Antichrist, receives a deadly head wound and is miraculously healed imitating the death and resurrection of Jesus Christ. The second beast, the False Prophet, creates an image of the Antichrist forces everyone to worship the image. The False Prophet will also force everyone to receive a mark in their forehead or right hand. The popular understanding of this mark is the RFID chip implanted under the skin. Since the False Prophet imitates Elijah by calling fire down from heaven, he will have little resistance in gathering believers to follow the Antichrist. If the Antichrist is a Muslim as I believe, he will immediately have millions of followers around the world.

The only points in the traditional paradigm that I would clarify are as follows:

- o The deadly head wound happens to one of the seven heads which represent kingdoms. This deadly wound happened to the Ottoman Caliphate in 1924 but will be healed when the Caliphate is re-established. I don't believe this deadly wound happens to a person, but I could be wrong.
- o If the Antichrist is killed and raised from the dead, then Satan is a giver of life and that is not possible.
- o No person can buy or sell without the mark, OR the name of the beast, OR the number of his name. Does the RFID chip cover all three? No

*"And he causeth all, both small and great, rich and poor, free and bond, to receive a mark in their **right hand**, or in their **foreheads**:"* — *Revelation 13:16*

What is the MARK?

Mark – Strongs G5480 - charagma *khar'-ag-mah* from the same as 5482; a scratch or etching, i.e. stamp (as **a badge of servitude**), or sculptured figure (statue):—graven, mark.

A badge of servitude to the beast kingdom makes more sense than an RFID chip for the RFID chip has no religious significance. However, a badge of servitude is an outward sign of allegiance to a god, kingdom, or person.

Isn't the mark "666"? Many people have used numerology to convert the names of various world leaders to a number. However, numerology is an occult practice and forbidden in scripture and, as you will see, completely unnecessary.

Let's go back to the beginning, or close to it. Below is the image of the text commonly translated as "666." This image is from Codex Vaticanus circa 350 A.D.

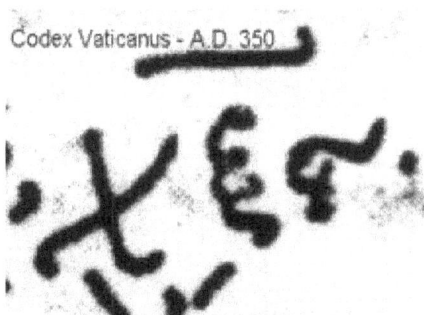

Codex Vaticanus - A.D. 350

I must give credit where credit is due. The below interpretation was discovered by Walid Shoebat, a former PLO terrorist converted to Christ and revealed in his book "God's War on Terror." As a Muslim trained in Arabic and the teachings of Islam, he immediately recognized the symbols in the codex as Arabic.

According to Walid, the first symbol (read from the right) is Arabic for "in the name of".

The middle symbol of the codex is the name "Allah" as can be easily seen in this script.

Below is a comparison between the Greek number 666 and the Name of Allah.

Greek 666:

Name of Allah:

93

The symbol on the left in both images is the crossed swords of Jihad. The middle symbol is the name Allah. The right symbol means "in the name of".

So, what is the mark or the badge of servitude? Could it be the head band worn by Muslim fundamentalists on their forehead or right arm. This badge of servitude identifies them with Allah and only worn by those loyal to Jihad. Also, it is worn by choice. Below is a Hamas headband.

The yellow headband of Hezbollah.

The Antichrist's followers can also be identified by the "number of his name." "number" - Strongs G706 – "arithmos", an indefinite number, a multitude (alternative interpretation from Strongs).

Instead of the Antichrist having a number, what if he has a multitude associated with his name? Is there a name in the Muslim world that has a multitude associated with it? Of course; Mohammed. What if the Antichrist was a direct descendent of Mohammed. Could he claim this multitude? Probably so.

How would Revelation 13:18 read using the alternate meaning of the words previously discussed? Paraphrase: "Here is wisdom. Let him that hath understanding reckon, discern the multitude of the beast: for it is the multitude of a man; and his multitude are (identified by) the name of Allah and the crossed swords of Jihad."

Many are already wearing the mark of the beast on their foreheads and right arms. Prior to 9/11 most people in the west paid little attention to the Middle East. That is slowly changing.

Does this alternate interpretation bear any witness in Scripture? Is there a "multitude" associated with the Antichrist/Mahdi?

*"And it shall come to pass in that day, that I will give unto Gog a place there of graves in Israel, the valley of the passengers on the east of the sea: and it shall stop the noses of the passengers: and there shall they bury Gog and all his **multitude**: and they shall call it The valley of Hamongog." — Ezekiel 39:11*

*"**Multitudes, multitudes** in the valley of decision: for the day of the LORD is near in the valley of decision." — Joel 3:14*

*"And he saith unto me, The waters which thou sawest, where the whore sitteth, are peoples, and **multitudes**, and nations, and tongues." — Rev 17:15*

These are just a few verses that associate a multitude with the battle of Armageddon and the Antichrist.

The alternate interpretation is extremely compatible with end time Scriptures and portrays the enemies of Israel as we see them continually in the news with headbands and armbands. Also, there is nothing religious about a computer chip but there is a direct religious association with the various Muslim headbands. No one wears a Muslim headband save those that worship Allah. As Islam is the religion of the spirit of Antichrist and its followers wear the mark (headband) of servitude to Allah, their names are not written in the Lamb's Book of Life thereby condemning them to the lake of fire.

Pärt Şĕvĕn

Ğäspĕl äf Mätthĕw

Ċhäptĕr Thirtĕĕn

Thĕ Ğäspĕl äf thĕ Kinğdäm

The Gospel of Matthew proclaims Jesus as King of the Jews and was written from a completely Jewish perspective as we will see. We are going to review the gospel for its Prophetic significance.

The Gospel of Matthew opens with the "genealogy of Jesus Christ, the son of David, the son of Abraham." This lineage validates His kingship as all kings come from the line of Judah.

The Gospel of the Kingdom was preached. Beginning in chapter 3 we read that John the Baptist preached the Gospel of the Kingdom *"repent for the kingdom of heaven is at hand."* This was a simple gospel (good news) of repent for the kingdom of heaven is here, the King is among us.

In Matthew, chapter 4 we read that after Jesus was tempted in the wilderness he went to Capernaum of Galilee (v. 12-13). In verse 17 we read *"From that time Jesus began to preach, and to say, **Repent; for the kingdom of heaven is at hand.**"*

After calling Peter, Andrew, James, and John to follow Him and become fishers of men, we read in verse 23, "And Jesus went about all Galilee, teaching in their synagogues, and *preaching the gospel of the kingdom…"*

In chapter 9:35 again we read, "And Jesus went about all the cities and villages, teaching in their synagogues, and preaching the **gospel of the kingdom**, and healing every sickness and every disease among the people."

In chapter 10 Jesus gathers the twelve and sends them out to preach to the Jews only. He instructs the disciples not to go into any Gentile city. Verse 7 reads, *"And as ye go, preach, saying,* **The kingdom of heaven is at hand.**"

"These twelve Jesus sent forth, and commanded them, saying, **Go not into the way of the Gentiles**, *and into any city of the Samaritans enter ye not: But go rather to the* **lost sheep of the house of Israel.** *And as ye go, preach, saying,* **The kingdom of heaven is at hand**." – Matthew 10:5-7*

However, the King and His Kingdom were rejected. In chapter 12, the Pharisees reject Jesus and blaspheme the Holy Spirit.

"Then was brought unto him one possessed with a devil, blind, and dumb: and he healed him, insomuch that the blind and dumb both spake and saw. And all the people were amazed, and said, Is not this the son of David? But when the Pharisees heard it, they said, **This fellow doth not cast out devils, but by Beelzebub the prince of the devils**.*" — Matthew 12:22-24*

Pharisees demand a sign from Jesus, but none was given except the promise of the sign of Jonah.

"But he answered and said unto them, An **evil and adulterous generation seeketh after a sign**; *and there shall no sign be given to it, but the sign of the prophet Jonas:* **For as Jonas was three days and three nights in the whale's belly; so shall the Son of man be three**

days and three nights in the heart of the earth." — Matthew
12:39-40

Jesus had proven himself the Messiah, but the rulers of
Israel continually rejected him. With the rejection of Jesus as
Messiah, it became clear that the Kingdom was no longer at
hand and for the next ten chapters the gospel of the Kingdom is
not mentioned in scripture.

Jesus then preached the kingdom of heaven parables
some alluding to a long period of time until the Kingdom would
be   restored to Israel. The kingdom of heaven is a physical
kingdom yet to come.

The disciples noticed the abrupt change and asked Jesus
why the sudden change in teaching methods.

And the disciples came, and said unto him, **Why speakest thou unto
them in parables?** *He answered and said unto them,* **Because it is
given unto you to know the mysteries of the kingdom of heaven,
but to them it is not given.** *For whosoever hath, to him shall be
given, and he shall have more abundance: but whosoever hath not,
from him shall be taken away even that he hath. Therefore speak I to
them in parables,* **because they seeing, see not; and hearing, they
hear not, neither do they understand.** *And in them is fulfilled the
prophecy of Esaias, which saith, By hearing ye shall hear, and shall
not understand; and seeing ye shall see, and shall not perceive: For
this* **people's heart is become gross, and their ears are dull of
hearing,** *and their eyes they have closed, lest at any time they should
see with their eyes, and hear with their ears, and should understand
with their heart, and should be converted, and I should heal them."* —
Matthew 13:10-15

The kingdom of heaven parables are wholly Jewish in
nature as is the entire Gospel of Matthew. The wheat and tares

parable pertains to the last days, the second coming of Jesus Christ.

We are given the interpretation of the wheat and tares parable. The other parables should be interpreted in like manner.

The wheat and tares parable:

*"Another parable put he forth unto them, saying, The kingdom of heaven is likened unto a **man which sowed good seed** in his field: But while **men slept**, his enemy came and **sowed tares among the wheat**, and went his way. But when the blade was sprung up, and brought forth fruit, then appeared the tares also. So the servants of the householder came and said unto him, Sir, didst not thou sow good seed in thy field? from whence then hath it tares? He said unto them, **An enemy hath done this**. The servants said unto him, Wilt thou then that we go and gather them up? But he said, Nay; lest while ye gather up the tares, ye root up also the wheat with them. **Let both grow together until the harvest**: and in the time of harvest I will say to the reapers, **Gather ye together first the tares, and bind them in bundles to burn them: but gather the wheat into my barn.**"* — *Matthew 13:24–30*

Interpretation given by Jesus:

*"Then Jesus sent the multitude away, and went into the house: and his disciples came unto him, saying, **Declare unto us the parable of the tares of the field**. He answered and said unto them, He that soweth the good seed is the Son of man; The field is the world; the good seed are the children of the kingdom; but the tares are the children of the wicked one; The enemy that sowed them is the devil; the harvest is the end of the world; and the reapers are the angels. As therefore the tares are gathered and burned in the fire; so shall it be in the end of this world. The Son of man shall send forth his angels, and*

they shall gather out of his kingdom all things that offend, and them which do iniquity; And shall cast them into a furnace of fire: there shall be wailing and gnashing of teeth. Then shall the righteous shine forth as the sun in the kingdom of their Father. Who hath ears to hear, let him hear." — Matthew 13:36-43

- o The sower of the good seed is the Son of Man, Jesus.
- o The field is the world.
- o The good seed are the children of the kingdom, Jews.
- o The tares are the children of the wicked one, the devil.
- o The enemy that sowed the tares was the devil.
- o The harvest is at the end of the age, the second coming.
- o The reapers are the angels.
- o The tares are gathered up and burned in the fire at the end of the age (not the church age but the Tribulation)
- o The Son of Man shall send angels to gather out of His kingdom all things that offend.
- o He shall cast them (tares) into a furnace of fire and there shall be wailing and gnashing of teeth (Hell).
- o This happens at the Lord's second coming at the end of the great tribulation as He sets up His kingdom to reign for 1000 years.
- o Then shall the righteous (wheat) shall shine forth as the sun in the kingdom of their Father.

"Fear not, little flock; for it is your **Father's good pleasure to give you the kingdom.**" - Luke 12:32 KJV. The "little flock," believing Jews, receive the kingdom.

Matthew chapter 24:

*"And Jesus went out, and departed from the temple: and his disciples came to him for to shew him the buildings of the temple. And Jesus said unto them, See ye not all these things? verily I say unto you, **There shall not be left here one stone upon another, that shall not be***

*thrown down. And as he sat upon the mount of Olives, the disciples came unto him privately, saying, Tell us, **when** shall these things be? and **what** shall be the **sign of thy coming**, and of the **end of the world**? And Jesus answered and said unto them, **Take heed that no man deceive you**.*" — *Matthew 24:1-4*

Jesus foretells the destruction of the temple, and the disciples question Him with; "when shall these things be? And what shall be the sign of thy coming, and of the end of the age?"

The "when" question was fulfilled in 70 A.D. when the Roman 10th legion destroyed Jerusalem and the Temple as recorded by Luke in chapter 21.

Jesus answers the "what" question in the remainder of chapter 24 thru 25.

*"For many shall come in my name, saying, **I am Christ**; and shall deceive many. And ye shall hear of **wars and rumours of wars**: see that ye be not troubled: for all these things must come to pass, but the end is not yet. For **nation shall rise against nation**, and kingdom against kingdom: and there shall be **famines, and pestilences**, and earthquakes, in divers places. All these are **the beginning of sorrows**. Then shall they deliver you up to be afflicted, and shall **kill you**: and ye shall be hated of all nations for my name's sake."* — *Matthew 24:5-9*

Compare these verses with Revelation chapter 6 and notice that the beginning of sorrows defined above is synonymous with the first five seals of Revelation 6. The Olivet Discourse (Matthew 24 & 25) and Revelation chapters 6 through 19 cover the same period, the 7-year tribulation.

Matthew 24	Revelation 6
v. 5 False Christ's (spirit of Antichrist)	1st Seal – White horse, Antichrist revealed
v. 6 Wars and rumors of wars	2nd Seal – Red horse – make war
v. 7 Famine	3rd Seal – Black horse - famine
v. 7 Pestilences, earthquakes	4th Seal – Pale horse - death
v. 9 Saints killed for His name's sake	5th Seal – Martyred souls under the altar

Matthew 24 and Revelation chapters 6 through 19 describe the Tribulation period at the end of the age. This is synonymous with the 70th week of Daniel prophesy; the 7-year tribulation (Dan 9:27). A seven-year period of judgment that falls upon a Christ rejecting world and a Christ rejecting Israel.

Beginning of Sorrows:

*"Howl ye; for the **day of the LORD is at hand**; it shall come as a **destruction from the Almighty**. Therefore shall all hands be faint, and every man's heart shall melt: And they shall be afraid: pangs and **sorrows** shall take hold of them; they shall be in pain as a **woman that travaileth:** they shall be amazed one at another; their faces shall be as flames." – Isaiah 13:6-8*

Daniel 9:27 – Matthew 24-25 – Revelation 6-19 each give an increasing number of details for the SAME SEVEN YEAR PERIOD at the end of the age when the Lord Jesus judges the earth and returns to set up His kingdom.

*"And then shall many be offended, and shall betray one another, and shall hate one another. And many False Prophets shall rise, and shall deceive many. And because iniquity shall abound, the love of many shall wax cold. **But he that shall endure unto the end, the same shall be saved. And this gospel of the kingdom shall be preached in***

all the world for a witness unto all nations; and then shall the end come." — Matthew 24:10-14

"*But he that shall endure unto the end, the same shall be saved.*" This statement cannot apply to us, the body of Christ, as we believers in Christ do not need to continue to the end of anything to know that we are saved. This can only apply to those living during the seven-year tribulation; if they continue (in their profession of faith in Christ) to the end they will be saved and enter the Millennial Kingdom. If they fall and follow the Antichrist they will be lost forever.

*"And they overcame him by the blood of the Lamb, and by the word of their testimony; and **they loved not their lives unto the death**."*
— Rev 12:11

In other words, the tribulation saints endured in their testimony even unto death to be saved.

In v. 24:14 notice that Jesus states; "*And this gospel of the kingdom shall be preached in all the world for a witness unto all nations; and then the end shall come.*" This is the very same gospel that Jesus and John the Baptist preached in the early chapters of the gospel of Matthew. This is NOT the gospel of grace that we now preach in this present dispensation of grace.

The preaching of the gospel of the kingdom ended during Jesus' ministry. He was rejected by the rulers of Israel therefore the kingdom was no longer "at hand". The gospel of grace began with the revelation given to the apostle Paul after his Damascus Road conversion (Acts 9) and will continue until the Rapture of the Church.

Then, during the seven-year tribulation period, the gospel of the kingdom will be preached again because the kingdom will, once again, be "at hand".

The gospel of grace and the gospel of the kingdom are mutually exclusive. The gospel of the kingdom is under the covenant of Moses and the gospel of grace is founded in the blood of Christ.

*"For the **law** was given by Moses, but **grace** and truth came by Jesus Christ." - John 1:17 KJV*

This is a crucial distinction that demands the removal (Rapture) of the Church prior to be beginning of the 7-year tribulation (70th week of Daniel's prophecy) so the gospel of the kingdom can once again be preached.

*"When ye therefore shall see the **abomination of desolation, spoken of by Daniel the prophet, stand in the holy place**, (whoso readeth, let him understand:) Then let them which be in Judaea flee into the mountains: Let him which is on the housetop not come down to take any thing out of his house: Neither let him which is in the field return back to take his clothes. And woe unto them that are with child, and to them that give suck in those days! But pray ye that your flight be not in the winter, neither on the sabbath day: For then shall be **great tribulation, such as was not since the beginning of the world to this time, no, nor ever shall be.** And except those days should be shortened, there should no flesh be saved: but for the **elect's sake** those days shall be shortened." — Matthew 24:15-22*

The abomination of desolation spoken by the prophet Daniel is first mentioned in Daniel chapter 9 and occurs in the midst (middle) of the 70th week, the 7-year Tribulation. We see a type of the abomination of desolation in Daniel chapter 11:31. In chapter 12:11 Daniel also mentions the abomination of desolation. Since Daniel states that the abomination of desolation occurs in the middle of the 7-year tribulation, then these verses in Matthew describe the middle of the 7-year tribulation.

This entire scenario is completely Jewish. The Antichrist stops the daily offering in the Temple to set up his image. Also, the Jews are told to pray that their exit from Jerusalem is not on the Sabbath since the Sabbath has travel restrictions. Since the

105

Church does not offer animal sacrifices and does not observe the Sabbath (Friday evening through Saturday evening) the context is therefore completely Jewish.

*"Then if any man shall say unto you, Lo, here is Christ, or there; believe it not. For **there shall arise false Christs, and False Prophets, and shall shew great signs and wonders**; insomuch that, if it were possible, they shall deceive the very elect. Behold, I have told you before. Wherefore if they shall say unto you, Behold, **he is in the desert**; go not forth: behold, he is in the **secret chambers**; believe it not. For as the **lightning cometh out of the east, and shineth even unto the west; so shall also the coming of the Son of man be.** For whersoever the carcase is, there will the eagles be gathered together."* — *Matthew 24:23-28*

Many false Christs and prophets will arise and try to deceive many, but the true Christ will come suddenly from heaven, and everyone will see that event. Why would Jesus issue a warning of a False Prophet being in the desert? What important Islamic city is in the desert? Mecca. What false Christ will come forth from Mecca? The Mahdi, the Islamic Messiah. More on him later.

*"**Immediately after the tribulation of those days shall the sun be darkened, and the moon shall not give her light,** and the stars shall fall from heaven, and the powers of the heavens shall be shaken: And then shall appear the **sign of the Son of man in heaven**: and then shall all the tribes of the earth mourn, and **they shall see the Son of man coming in the clouds of heaven with power and great glory.** And he shall send his angels with a great sound of a trumpet, and they shall **gather together his elect from the four winds, from one end of heaven to the other.**"* — *Matthew 24:29-31*

*"Ho, ho, come forth, and flee from the land of the north, saith the LORD: for I have spread you abroad as **the four winds of the heaven**, saith the LORD."* — *Zechariah 2:6*

At the end of the 3 ½ year period of great tribulation; the second half of the 7-year tribulation period; the earth will be in such calamity that the sun is darkened, and the moon will not give any light due to warfare and natural disasters. As Israel is on the brink of destruction, Jesus will appear in the clouds of heaven with power and great glory. The four winds of heaven refer to the Jew being scattered in every direction and gathered again. This gathering has nothing to do with the rapture of the Church. Those gathered at that time are Jews that will enter the Millennial Kingdom.

*"Now learn a parable of the **fig tree**; When his branch is yet tender, and putteth forth leaves, ye know that summer is nigh: So likewise ye, **when ye shall see all these things, know that it is near, even at the doors.** Verily I say unto you, **This generation shall not pass, till all these things be fulfilled.** Heaven and earth shall pass away, but my words shall not pass away."* — *Matthew 24:32–35*

The generation that sees the signs, the birth pangs, will not pass (die) until all these things are fulfilled (completed). The generation that sees the stage being set for this last day's period of seven years will see its completion. We are that generation.

*"But of **that day and hour knoweth no man**, no, not the angels of heaven, but my Father only. **But as the days of Noe were, so shall also the coming of the Son of man be.** For as in the days that were **before the flood** they were eating and drinking, marrying and giving in marriage, until the day that Noe entered into the ark, **And knew not until the flood came, and took them all away; so shall also the coming of the Son of man be. Then** shall two be in the field; the **one***

shall be taken, and the other left. *Two women shall be grinding at the mill; the* **one shall be taken, and the other left.** **Watch therefore:** *for ye know not what hour your Lord doth come.* *But know this, that if the goodman of the house had known in what watch the thief would come, he would have watched, and would not have suffered his house to be broken up.* **Therefore be ye also ready: for in such an hour as ye think not the Son of man cometh.**" — *Matthew 24:36-44*

"That day and hour knoweth no man..." is a very precise phrase. The Lord did not use year, decade, century, or month. The precision of the language shows that those watching will know the time and season.

The coming of the Son of Man will be like the days of Noah. They were living their lives but did not believe Noah about the coming destruction. They did not understand until the flood came and took them away. Who did the flood take away? It took away the unbelievers; those that did not believe the truth that Noah preached for all those decades while building the ark.

Then shall two be in the field, one taken one left. The word "then" brings the concept of the previous verses about Noah's flood forward to the second coming. Unbelievers will be taken away at Jesus' second coming since they have no love for the truth. They will be unaware of the pending destruction. Then, at the coming of the Lord, two will in the field, one taken (taken away in unbelief) and one left. The one taken away is an unbeliever taken away to judgment. The one left is a believer who will enter the kingdom.

This also is the fulfillment of the parable of the wheat and tares. The angels will gather all unbelievers (seed of the evil one - tares) and cast them in the fire of hell. All things that offend the Lord Jesus Christ will be removed from the earth.

This is NOT the Rapture of the Church as some say it is. This is the separation of the wheat and tares. The "one taken" is removed and cast into the fire of hell. The "one left" will enter the kingdom for this event happens at the coming of the Jesus

Christ; exactly the opposite of the rapture. At the rapture of the Church, the believers are taken away to heaven and the unbelievers remain to suffer the seven-year tribulation.

This is an excellent example of how staying in context will define and explain the scripture. The context is the Second Coming of Jesus. The destiny of unbelievers at that time is just like what happened to the unbelievers at the time of Noah's flood. They were removed from the earth to an eternity in the fires of hell.

*"Who then is **a faithful and wise servant**, whom his lord hath made ruler over his household, to give them meat in due season? Blessed is that servant, whom his lord when he cometh **shall find so doing**. Verily I say unto you, That **he shall make him ruler over all his goods**. But and if that evil servant shall say in his heart, My lord delayeth his coming; And shall begin to smite his fellowservants, and to eat and drink with the drunken; The lord of that servant shall come in a day when he looketh not for him, and in an hour that he is not aware of, And shall cut him asunder, and appoint him his portion with the hypocrites: there shall be weeping and gnashing of teeth."* – *Matthew 24:45-51*

The evil servant is in rebellion against his master; he is an unbeliever. He will be cast out to a place of weeping and gnashing of teeth. The servants that do the will of the master are rewarded. This is the same message as the "days of Noah verses." Watch and be ready.

Matthew chapter 25:

*"Then shall the kingdom of heaven **be likened** unto ten virgins, which took their lamps, and went forth to meet the bridegroom. And five of them were wise, and five were foolish. They that were foolish took their lamps, and took no oil with them: But the wise took oil in their vessels with their lamps. While the bridegroom tarried, they all*

slumbered and slept. And at midnight there was a cry made, Behold, the bridegroom cometh; go ye out to meet him. Then all those virgins arose, and trimmed their lamps. And the foolish said unto the wise, Give us of your oil; for our lamps are gone out. But the wise answered, saying, Not so; lest there be not enough for us and you: but go ye rather to them that sell, and buy for yourselves. And while they went to buy, the bridegroom came; and they that were ready went in with him to the marriage: and the door was shut. Afterward came also the other virgins, saying, Lord, Lord, open to us. But he answered and said, Verily I say unto you, I know you not. **Watch therefore, for ye know neither the day nor the hour wherein the Son of man cometh.**" *— Matthew 25:1-13*

Ten virgins are pictured, five wise, five foolish. They are waiting for the bridegroom, but they are not the bride for they are only invited to the marriage supper (kingdom). The ten virgins are the Jewish at the second coming of the Lord. Five are prepared for the kingdom (the faithful remnant), five are not prepared (apostate Israel). It is just that simple. Be careful not to read too much symbolism into parables.

The oil that the foolish five were sent to buy is not the Holy Spirit for He is not for sale. Watch, for you know not when the Son of man cometh (Second Coming of the Lord).

"For the kingdom of heaven is **as** *a man travelling into a far country, who called his own servants, and delivered unto them his goods. And unto one he gave five talents, to another two, and to another one; to every man according to his several ability; and straightway took his journey. Then he that had received the five talents went and traded with the same, and made them other five talents. And likewise he that had received two, he also gained other two. But he that had received one went and digged in the earth, and* **hid his lord's money.** **After a long time the lord of those servants cometh,** *and reckoneth*

with them. And so he that had received five talents came and brought other five talents, saying, Lord, thou deliveredst unto me five talents: behold, I have gained beside them five talents more. His lord said unto him, **Well done***, thou good and faithful servant: thou hast been faithful over a few things, I will make thee ruler over many things: enter thou into the joy of thy lord. He also that had received two talents came and said, Lord, thou deliveredst unto me two talents: behold, I have gained two other talents beside them. His lord said unto him,* **Well done***, good and faithful servant; thou hast been faithful over a few things, I will make thee ruler over many things: enter thou into the joy of thy lord. Then he which had received the one talent came and said, Lord, I knew thee that thou art an hard man, reaping where thou hast not sown, and gathering where thou hast not strawed: And I was afraid, and went and hid thy talent in the earth: lo, there thou hast that is thine. His lord answered and said unto him, Thou wicked and slothful servant, thou knewest that I reap where I sowed not, and gather where I have not strawed: Thou oughtest therefore to have put my money to the exchangers, and then at my coming I should have received mine own with usury. Take therefore the talent from him, and give it unto him which hath ten talents.* **For unto every one that hath shall be given, and he shall have abundance: but from him that hath not shall be taken away even that which he hath.** *And cast ye the unprofitable servant into outer darkness: there shall be weeping and gnashing of teeth."*
— *Matthew 24:13-30*

This is also a parable proclaiming that while the Lord tarries during the 7-year Tribulation the Jews must be about His business doing His will. Those that do not His will are cast into hell. That parable has nothing to do with us, the body of Christ.

"When the Son of man shall come in his glory, *and all the holy angels with him, then shall he sit upon the throne of his glory: And* **before**

111

him shall be gathered all nations: and he shall separate them one from another, as a shepherd divideth his sheep from the goats: And he shall set the sheep on his right hand, but the goats on the left. Then shall the King say unto them on his right hand, Come, ye blessed of my Father, inherit the kingdom prepared for you from the foundation of the world: For I was an hungred, and ye gave me meat: I was thirsty, and ye gave me drink: I was a stranger, and ye took me in: Naked, and ye clothed me: I was sick, and ye visited me: I was in prison, and ye came unto me. Then shall the righteous answer him, saying, Lord, when saw we thee an hungred, and fed thee? or thirsty, and gave thee drink? When saw we thee a stranger, and took thee in? or naked, and clothed thee? Or when saw we thee sick, or in prison, and came unto thee? And the King shall answer and say unto them, Verily I say unto you, **Inasmuch as ye have done it unto one of the least of these my brethren, ye have done it unto me.** Then shall he say also unto them on the left hand, Depart from me, ye cursed, into everlasting fire, prepared for the devil and his angels: For I was an hungred, and ye gave me no meat: I was thirsty, and ye gave me no drink: I was a stranger, and ye took me not in: naked, and ye clothed me not: sick, and in prison, and ye visited me not. Then shall they also answer him, saying, Lord, when saw we thee an hungred, or athirst, or a stranger, or naked, or sick, or in prison, and did not minister unto thee? Then shall he answer them, saying, **Verily I say unto you, Inasmuch as ye did it not to one of the least of these, ye did it not to me. And these shall go away into everlasting punishment: but the righteous into life eternal.**" — Matthew 24:32-46*

At the coming of the Son of Man, all nations will be gathered before him. Nations (peoples) are separated as sheep and goats (wheat and tares). The Sheep (righteous wheat) are on His right hand and the goats (unrighteous tares) on His left hand.

The sheep are judged righteous and inherit the kingdom. The goats are cast into everlasting fire prepared for the devil and his angels. The judgment is based on how they treated Jesus' brethren, the Jew, during the Tribulation.

This judgment has nothing to do with the Church. It determines who will enter the 1000-year reign of Christ as humans that will repopulate the earth after the terrible destruction of the great tribulation.

At that time the Church, being raptured 7-years prior, are all in glorified bodies and with the Lord at this judgment. Matthew chapters 24 and 25 pertain to the 7-year tribulation and are completely Jewish, the Church is not involved. Many preachers and teachers try to apply these verses to the Church creating confusion and misunderstanding. Remember that the Book of Matthew is to the Jew and not the Church. Leave the Church out of Matthew, apply the teachings to the Jew and the confusion will disappear.

Part Eight

The Gathering

Chapter Fourteen

First Thessalonians

1st Thessalonians was written by the Apostle Paul while at Corinth on his second missionary journey. In the first three chapters Paul is validating his ministry and giving them instructions on proper Christian living. During that time there was an intense belief that Jesus would return at any moment. However, after some time passed several believers had died (sleep). Those still alive questioned Paul as to what would happen to the dead believers at Christ's coming. Paul answers the question beginning in chapter 4 verse 13.

*"But I would not have you to be ignorant, brethren, **concerning them which are asleep,** that ye **sorrow not,** even as others which have no hope. For if we believe that Jesus **died and rose again,** even so them also which sleep in Jesus **will God bring with him.** For this we say unto you by the word of the Lord, that we which are alive and remain unto the coming of the Lord shall not prevent them which are asleep. For the Lord himself shall descend from heaven with a **shout,** with the **voice of the archangel,** and with the **trump of God**: and the **dead in Christ shall rise first:** Then we which are alive and remain **shall be caught up together with them in the clouds, to meet the***

Lord in the air: *and so shall we ever be with the Lord. Wherefore comfort one another with these words." — 1ˢᵗ Thessalonians 4:13-18*

Paul gives the answer "concerning them which are asleep." Just as Jesus "died and rose again" so those that sleep in Jesus will do the same. At Christ's return for believers at the rapture, the dead will rise first then we who are alive will join them in the clouds and meet the Lord in the air. From then on, we shall always be with the Lord.

This is the catching away of believers, living and dead, commonly referred to as the rapture of the Church. It involves believers in Christ only during this present dispensation of Grace.

We meet the Lord in the air. Jesus does not come to the land as described in Zechariah where He descends upon the Mount of Olives and it cleaves in half. Instead, at the rapture the Lord comes in the air for His church; He does not rescue Israel and fight her enemies in the land.

Therefore, this event is unique and totally different from the Second Coming of Christ (the Day of the Lord).

Rapture positions with reference to the tribulation:
1. **Pre-trib** – the rapture occurs prior to the 7-year tribulation.
2. **Mid-trib** – the rapture occurs at the middle of the tribulation just prior to the 3 ½ years of great tribulation.
3. **Pre-wrath** – the rapture will occur later in the 7-year tribulation but before the wrath of God is poured out upon the earth.
4. **Post-trib** – the rapture occurs at the time of the Second Coming of Christ.

Many criticize the pre-tribulation rapture position as escapism mentality. However, that is just what Paul said; we will escape the terrible things to come. Even though that verse is for

Israel during the tribulation, we in the church should continually be looking for the rapture. There are many great websites and books that list the many reasons for the accuracy of the pre-tribulation rapture position, so I see no need to list them here. However, there are a few points I would like to mention.

Those that hold to the Mid-tribulation, Pre-wrath, or Post-tribulation rapture position are actually looking for the Antichrist and not the Lord Jesus Christ. In those views the Antichrist must come, and the seven-year tribulation begin before the rapture takes place. This destroys the concept of the imminent return of Jesus Christ taught in the Word and by countless saints down through the ages. We are to be ready for the blessed hope, the return of Jesus in the rapture.

"For the grace of God that bringeth salvation hath appeared to all men, Teaching us that, denying ungodliness and worldly lusts, we should live soberly, righteously, and godly, in this present world; **Looking for that blessed hope, and the glorious appearing of the great God and our Saviour Jesus Christ;"** *— Titus 2:11-13*

"But of the times and the seasons, brethren, **ye** *have no need that I write unto* **you**. *For yourselves know perfectly that the* **day of the Lord so cometh as a thief in the night**. *For when* **they** *shall say,* **Peace and safety; then sudden destruction cometh upon them, as travail upon a woman with child;** *and* **they** *shall not escape. But* **ye,** *brethren, are* **not in darkness, that that day should overtake you as a thief.** *Ye are all the children of light, and the children of the day:* **we** *are not of the night, nor of darkness. Therefore let* **us** *not sleep, as do others; but let* **us** *watch and be sober. For* **they** *that sleep sleep in the night; and* **they** *that be drunken are drunken in the night. But let* **us,** *who are of the day, be sober, putting on the breastplate of faith and love; and for an helmet, the hope of salvation.* **For God hath not appointed us to wrath, but to obtain salvation by our Lord Jesus Christ,** *Who died for us, that, whether we wake or sleep, we should*

live together with him. Wherefore comfort yourselves together, and edify one another, even as also ye do." — 1 Thes 5:1-11

I have highlighted the pronouns (ye, we, us, and they) in this text so you can easily contrast "they" and "us". "They" will not escape; "We and us" escape via the rapture.

Paul had obviously given believers a thorough teaching on the rapture and second coming with the words "you know perfectly well". Paul states clearly that the Day of the Lord so comes as a thief in the night. That is the second coming at the end of the 7-year tribulation. We can verify this in Rev 16.

"Behold, I come as a thief. *Blessed is he that watcheth, and keepeth his garments, lest he walk naked, and they see his shame. And he gathered them together into a place called in the Hebrew tongue* **Armageddon**." — *Rev 16:15-16*

We believers do not dwell in darkness that the Day of the Lord should overtake us. Our God has not appointed us to wrath but to obtain salvation (deliverance) by our Lord Jesus Christ (in the rapture).

Crucial Point of Understanding:

Since we have now covered the Rapture of the Church and the 70 Week Prophecy in Daniel chapter 9, I want to make a point about the covenant. The entire 70 weeks (490 years) of Daniels prophecy (Daniel 9:24-27) was given under the covenant of Moses. We have seen the gap between the 69th and 70th week of the prophecy. In that gap Jesus was crucified and the Romans destroyed the Temple in Jerusalem.

The 70th week begins when the Antichrist confirms a 7-year covenant with Israel. Since that has not happened at the time of this writing, we are still in the gap between the 69th and 70th week of Daniels prophecy. In this gap we have the entire Church age, the dispensation of grace. The Church began in the gap. The Church age will end in the gap someday soon at the Rapture. The entire dispensation of grace occurs during the gap.

The Church is under the New Testament by the blood of Jesus Christ. We preach the gospel of grace. For the covenant of Moses to return for the 70th week to begin, the Church must be removed. God has never dealt with man via two covenants simultaneously.

The covenant of Moses and the dispensation of grace in the blood of Christ are not compatible. You cannot be under the law and under grace at the same time. The apostle Paul makes this point many times in his epistles of Romans, Corinthians, and Galatians.

*"For sin shall not have dominion over you: for ye are not **under the law**, but **under grace**." — Romans 6:14*

*"But if ye be led of the Spirit, ye are **not under the law**." — Galatians 5:18*

*"For Christ is the **end of the law** for righteousness to everyone that believeth." — Romans 10:4*

Also, these two paradigms have two different gospels: the gospel of the kingdom and the gospel of grace. What gospel is preached in Matthew chapter 24? The gospel of the kingdom is preached because the Jews are back under the covenant of Moses and Israel's prophetic kingdom program for the last 7-years of the 70-week prophecy of Daniel chapter 9.

Before the 70th week of Daniel can begin under the covenant of Moses, the Church must be removed. It is obvious from Matthew chapter 24 that the Jews are in the land of Israel because they are observing the daily Temple sacrifices and the Sabbath. These observances clearly reveal that the covenant of Moses is again active. Therefore the Church must be raptured before the 7-year tribulation begins. The Church must be removed from earth before the old covenant of Moses can be once again practiced in Israel and the coming Temple. Those that place the Rapture during or at the end of the tribulation period have two major issues. One, they have a faulty understanding of the Church of Jesus Christ. Two, they also have a misunderstanding of the purpose of the seven-year tribulation (the 70th week of Daniel's prophecy).

Chapter Fifteen

Second Thessalonians Chapter Two

*"Now we beseech you, brethren, by the coming of our Lord Jesus Christ, and by **our gathering together unto him,** That ye be not soon shaken in mind, or be troubled, neither by spirit, nor by word, nor by letter as from us, as that the **day of Christ is at hand.**"—2 Thes 2:1-2*

"Now we beseech you, brethren, by the coming of our Lord Jesus Christ, and by our gathering together unto him," – 2 Thessalonians 2:1 KJV. At first glance, one might think there are two topics here, "the coming of the Lord" and "our gathering together unto him." But that is not the case. We see this construct many times in the KJV, where two phrases are connected with an "and" or the word "even." The first phrase defines the topic, and the second phrase gives a descriptive characteristic of the topic. The "coming of the Lord" is for us "gathering together unto him." That is one event, the Rapture. That is the only future event where the Lord comes, and we believers, the Church, are gathered to meet Him. So, the context of the passage is set in verse 1 as the Rapture of the Church. Then we would logically expect Paul to mention the Rapture somewhere in the subsequent verses. Stating the context and not mentioning it again would be illogical and flawed literary style, something someone of Paul's education and intelligence would never do. Not to mention that the Holy Spirit, the Spirit of Truth, would never leave the reader with a vague, confusing, and incomplete concept.

"That ye be not soon shaken in mind, or be troubled, neither by spirit, nor by word, nor by letter as from us, as that the day of Christ is at hand." - 2Thessalonians 2:2 KJV. The believers in Thessalonica were shaken up. They were upset and troubled because they were told the Day of the Lord (the 7-year Tribulation) had begun. That was contrary to what Paul taught; otherwise, there would be no reason for them to be troubled. We do not know how they received this erroneous information, but it must have come from a credible source for them to write to Paul for clarification. It could have come by revelation from a demon spirit, or by word of mouth, or by a forged letter allegedly from the Apostle Paul himself. Either way, they were upset and wanted some clarification on the Rapture timeline.

"Let no man deceive you by any means: for that day shall not come, except there come a falling away first, and that man of sin be revealed, the son of perdition;" - 2Th 2:3 KJV. The verse opens with a stern warning, "let no man deceive you." In other words, if any man comes to you with a different Rapture scenario than the scenario Paul is about to give, he is a deceiver. That was true in Paul's day and still valid today. In our modern world, deception can come from many sources and in different forms. There are a great many "means" available for the devil's minions to perpetrate mass deception upon the Church. What the Thessalonians had heard about being in the Day of the Lord was a deception.

Paul clearly states an event must come "first" before the beginning of the Day of the Lord, the 7-year Tribulation, wherein the Antichrist, the son of perdition, is revealed. Remember, the Antichrist is revealed when he confirms the 7-year covenant that begins the Tribulation (Daniel 9:27). The 7-year Tribulation and the Day of the Lord in this context are synonymous. But what exactly is this "first" event that precedes the Tribulation?

The Greek word is "apostasia." It is rendered as "a falling away" in the KJV and most all modern Bibles. But was that the original intended meaning? As you can see in the table below, all the English Bibles (Wycliffe to Geneva) before the King James Version translated "apostasia" as "departing."

Year	Bible	Translation
382	Jerome's Latin Vulgate	Departure First
1384	Wycliffe Bible	Departynge First
1526	Tyndale Bible	Departynge First
1535	Coverdale Bible	Departynge First
1539	Crammer Bible	Departing First
1576	Breeches Bible	Departing First
1583	Beeza Bible	Departing First
1608	Geneva Bible	Departing First
1611	King James Bible	Falling Away

"Let no one deceive you in any way. For it will not be, unless the departure comes first, and the man of sin is revealed, the son of destruction," - 2Thess 2:3 HNV. Here in the modern Hebrew Names Version the word "apostasia" is translated as "the departure."

How's your Latin? "ne quis vos seducat ullo modo quoniam nisi venerit discessio primum et revelatus fuerit homo peccati filius perditionis" - 2Th 2:3 VUL. The phrase "discessio primum" means "departure first," St. Jerome's Latin Vulgate, 382 A.D. Since the earliest writings, "apostasia" had been translated as "departing" or "departure."

The Greek word "apostasia" is a combination of "apo," meaning "from" and "istemi," meaning "stand." It means to stand away from or departure. The word's context in our passage under investigation has nothing to do with falling away from the faith as the object departed from is not in the word meaning.

The Greek has the definite article before "apostasia" adding emphasis as "the departure" or "the departing." That means it is a reference back to a previous mention or teaching. If this were the first occurrence of this teaching, Paul would have used the indefinite article as "a departure." "the apostasia" is, therefore, a definitive event previously taught by Paul, the rapture from verse 1.

"Since the Greek language does not need an article to make the noun definite, it becomes clear that with the usage of

123

the article, reference is being made to something in particular. In 2 Thessalonians 2:3, the word apostasia is prefaced by the definite article, which means that Paul is pointing to a particular type of departure known to the Thessalonian church." Daniel K. Davey, "The 'Apostesia' of II Thessalonians 2:3," Th.M. thesis, Detroit Baptist Theological Seminary, May 1982, p. 47.

Paul is not introducing new teaching in verse 3 about a "spiritual departure," i.e., a falling away from the faith. He refers to a "physical departure" previously taught by him during his missionary visit to Thessalonica and in his first epistle to those believers.

"the departure" MUST be an event; otherwise, it would be impossible to know when it happened. A spiritual departure, a falling away from the faith, is not an event. It is a process, one that has been ongoing since the first century. There have always been areas falling away from the faith for various reasons and, at the same time, revivals happening elsewhere. It is impossible to date the starting and ending of a spiritual departure from the faith. The process is too indefinite and ambiguous. However, the Rapture is a specific event that happens very quickly, easily observable as a singular event.

Another point that needs to be made here is that Paul is not giving the primary teaching in this text. The direct instruction was given to the Thessalonian believers while Paul was with them. We are reading a second or follow-up conversation on the topic of the Rapture and the Day of the Lord in this passage. That is why Paul uses more common or familiar language because he references something he has already taught. He is using everyday words to refer to the primary teaching given while present with them. Words like "the departure" and "he who now restrains" are concepts previously taught by Paul, so he does not elaborate on them as he expects the believers in Thessalonica to remember his teachings and reference those words back to his primary teaching. We know this is the case as Paul states: "Remember ye not, that, when I was yet with you, I told you these things?" - 2Thessalonians 2:5 KJV.

There are three rules for acquiring a piece of real estate, whether for business or personal residence: location, location, location. Similarly, there are three rules for correct Bible interpretation: context, context, context. I can't stress this enough. If you depart from the context, you will fall into error. It is interesting and valuable to examine the Greek words and notice how the text was handled historically. Still, the passage's context is paramount and must be followed for any interpretation to be valid. In verse one, we noted that the passage's context is the Rapture of the Church, not a falling away from the faith. Therefore, the departure, the "apostasia," must refer to the Rapture, the physical departure of the Church. There is no other word in the passage that would refer to the Rapture context of verse one. Paul clearly states that the Rapture comes first, then the man of sin is revealed, which begins the Day of the Lord, the 7-year Tribulation. Here is a paraphrase of verse 3. "Let no man deceive you by any means: for the Day of the Lord, the 7-year Tribulation will not come, except there comes the departure, the Rapture first, and then that man of sin, the Antichrist is revealed, the son of perdition."

*"And now ye know what **withholdeth** that he might be revealed in his time. For the mystery of iniquity doth already work: only **he who now letteth will let, until he be taken out of the way**."* — *2 Thes 2:6-7*

There was and is something restraining the man of sin from being revealed before his time. The Holy Spirit working through the church during this present dispensation of grace, is the only entity on earth capable of restraining the mystery of iniquity and the man of sin. The mystery of iniquity is not open sin and rebellion against God for there is no mystery there and that continues daily. The mystery of iniquity is spiritual evil present in the world through deceivers, False Prophets and teachers espousing doctrines of demons, spiritual wickedness in high places culminating in Satan being manifest in the flesh as the Antichrist. This is why we war not against flesh and blood.

But at the right time, the Holy Spirit who restrains their full revelation will be taken out of the way. This will be at the rapture of the Church since we are the temple of the Holy Spirit, we are sealed with the Holy Spirit and when he goes, we go. The special presence of the Spirit as the indweller of saints will terminate abruptly at the rapture. Once the body of Christ has been caught away to heaven, the Spirit's ministry will revert back to what he did for believers during the Old Testament period wherein he came upon specific individuals for a specific ministry for a specific time period.

*"And **then shall that Wicked be revealed**, whom the Lord shall **consume** with the spirit of his mouth, and shall **destroy** with the brightness of his coming: Even him, **whose coming is after the working of Satan with all power and signs and lying wonders**, And with all **deceivableness of unrighteousness** in them that perish; **because they received not the love of the truth, that they might be saved.**" — 2 Thes 2:8-10*

That Wicked (Antichrist) is revealed after the rapture and destroyed 7-years later at the second coming of Jesus Christ. Revelation 13 foretells how Satan will give power and authority to the beast kingdom and the Antichrist. Satan empowers the Antichrist who deceives with power, signs and lying wonders all that have not received the love of the truth (Jesus).

*"And for this cause **God shall send them strong delusion, that they should believe a lie**: That they all might be damned who believed not the truth, but had pleasure in unrighteousness." — 2 Thes 2:11-12*

Those that have no love for the truth will be sent a strong delusion that they should believe the lie that the Antichrist is god. For this they will be damned. Also, they had pleasure in their sin; they loved the concept that man can become gods and we can control our destiny without God.

Chapter Sixteen

First Corinthians Chapter Fifteen

The relevance of the resurrection of Jesus:

*"Now if Christ be preached that he rose from the dead, how say some among you that there is **no resurrection of the dead**? But if there be no resurrection of the dead, then is Christ not risen:"* – 1 Cor 15:12-13

The Corinthian believers were being influenced by Greek philosophy holding to the concept that a spiritual existence in eternity was a superior state than being resurrected with a physical body. They were not denying the resurrection of Jesus just their own.

*"And **if Christ be not risen**, then is our preaching **vain**, and your faith is also **vain**. Yea, and we are found **false witnesses** of God; because we have testified of God that he raised up Christ: whom he raised not up, if so be that the dead rise not. For if the dead rise not, then is not Christ raised: And **if Christ be not raised, your faith is vain; ye are yet in your sins**. Then they also which are **fallen asleep in Christ are perished**. If in this life only we have hope in Christ, we are of all **men most miserable**."* — 1 Cor 15:14-19

Here are some conclusions about the resurrection of our Lord Jesus Christ:
- o If Christ is not risen, then our preaching is in vain.
- o If Christ is not risen, then we are found false witnesses of God.

- o If Christ is not risen, your faith is futile.
- o If Christ is not risen, you are still in your sins.
- o If Christ is not risen, then those who have fallen asleep in Christ have perished.
- o If Christ is not risen, then in this life only we have hope in Christ, and we are of all men the most pitiable. Christianity is then a pitiful joke!

See how important the truth of the resurrection is! The resurrection of Jesus Christ is the cornerstone of Christianity.

*"But now is Christ risen from the dead, and become the **firstfruits of them that slept**. For since by man came death, by man came also the resurrection of the dead. For as in Adam all die, even so in Christ shall all be made alive. **But every man in his own order: Christ the firstfruits; afterward they that are Christ's at his coming.**"* — 1 Cor 15:20-23

The offering at the Feast of Firstfruits was a bloodless grain offering (Leviticus 2). No atoning sacrifice was necessary, because the Passover lamb had just been sacrificed. This corresponds perfectly with the resurrection of Jesus because His death ended the need for sacrifice, having provided a perfect and complete atonement satisfying the justice of God.

*"And shall come forth; they that have done good, unto the **resurrection of life**; and they that have done evil, unto the **resurrection of damnation**."* — *John 5:29*

*"**Then cometh the end**, when he shall have **delivered up the kingdom to God, even the Father**; when he shall have **put down all rule** and all authority and power. For he must reign, till he hath put **all enemies under his feet**. The **last enemy that shall be destroyed is death**. For he hath **put all things under his feet**. But when he saith*

all things are put under him, it is manifest that he is excepted, which did put all things under him. And when all things shall be subdued unto him, then shall the Son also himself be subject unto him that put all things under him, that God may be all in all." — 1 Cor 15:24-28

- o Then comes the end when He delivers the kingdom to God the Father.
- o He puts an end to all rule and all authority and power.
- o He must reign till He has put all enemies under His feet.
- o The last enemy that will be destroyed is death.

Paul reminds us of something important: death is an enemy. When Jesus came to the tomb of Lazarus, He groaned in the spirit and was troubled, and Jesus wept (John 11:33, 35). Why? Not simply because Lazarus was dead, for Jesus would raise him shortly. Instead, Jesus was troubled at death itself. It was an enemy. Today, some are told to embrace death as a friend, but that is not Biblical thinking. Death is a defeated enemy because of the work of Jesus, an enemy that will one day be destroyed, and therefore an enemy we need not fear. But death is an enemy, nonetheless.

All things will then be put under Jesus' feet and the Son will be subject to the Father. Simply put, God the Father will always be God the Father, and God the Son will always be God the Son, and for all eternity they will continue to relate to each other as Father and Son.

*"Else what shall **they** do which are **baptized for the dead**, if the dead rise not at all? why are they then baptized for the dead? And **why stand we in jeopardy every hour?** I protest by your rejoicing which I have in Christ Jesus our Lord, I die daily. If after the manner of men I have fought with beasts at Ephesus, what advantageth it me, if the dead rise not? let us eat and drink; for tomorrow we die." — 1 Cor 15:29-32*

A pagan belief holds that you could be baptized for the dead. Mormons also practice this pagan belief. Paul is asking the question; if the pagans believe in the resurrection how much more should Christians believe?

Paul also asks; if there is no resurrection then why do we put our life in jeopardy every hour to preach the gospel? For the gospels sake I die daily. I have endured the afflictions of evil men at Ephesus for the sake of the gospel, but if there is no resurrection then why bother? Let's just eat, drink and be merry for tomorrow we might die.

*"**Be not deceived**: evil communications corrupt good manners. Awake to righteousness, and sin not; for some have not the knowledge of God: I speak this to your shame." – 1 Cor 15:33-34*

The Corinthians received the false doctrine of "no resurrection" from the local Hellenistic Jews and Greek philosophy. The believers were keeping evil company, and this will eventually corrupt other truths. Through much of his book, Paul deals with the moral problems of the Corinthians: envy, divisions, pride, immorality, greed, irreverence, and selfishness. How much of this had come in because of their keeping of evil company? Their problem with the resurrection was an indicator of the source of their moral problems also.

Awake to righteousness, do not be conformed to this world but be transformed by the renewing of your mind (Rom 12:20).

*But some man will say, **How are the dead raised up?** and with what body do they come? Thou fool, that which thou sowest is not quickened, except it die: And that which thou sowest, thou sowest not that body that shall be, but bare grain, it may chance of wheat, or of some other grain: But God giveth it a body as it hath pleased him, and to every seed his own body. All flesh is not the same flesh: but there is one kind of flesh of men, another flesh of beasts, another of*

132

fishes, and another of birds. There are also celestial bodies, and bodies terrestrial: but the glory of the celestial is one, and the glory of the terrestrial is another. There is one glory of the sun, and another glory of the moon, and another glory of the stars: for one star differeth from another star in glory. So also is the resurrection of the dead. It is sown in corruption; it is raised in incorruption: It is sown in dishonour; it is raised in glory: it is sown in weakness; it is raised in power: It is sown a natural body; it is raised a spiritual body. There is a natural body, and there is a spiritual body. And so it is written, The first man Adam was made a living soul; the last Adam was made a quickening spirit. And so it is written, The first man Adam was made a living soul; the last Adam was made a quickening spirit. Howbeit that was not first which is spiritual, but that which is natural; and afterward that which is spiritual. The first man is of the earth, earthy: the second man is the Lord from heaven. As is the earthy, such are they also that are earthy: and as is the heavenly, such are they also that are heavenly. And as we have borne the image of the earthy, we shall also bear the image of the heavenly." — 1 Cor 15:35-49

*"Now this I say, brethren, that **flesh and blood cannot inherit the kingdom of God**; neither doth corruption inherit incorruption. Behold, **I shew you a mystery; We shall not all sleep, but we shall all be changed, In a moment, in the twinkling of an eye, at the last trump: for the trumpet shall sound, and the dead shall be raised incorruptible, and we shall be changed**. For this corruptible must put on incorruption, and this mortal must put on immortality. So when this corruptible shall have put on incorruption, and this mortal shall have put on immortality, then shall be brought to pass the saying that is written, **Death is swallowed up in victory**. O death, where is thy sting? O grave, where is thy victory? The sting of death is sin; and the strength of sin is the law. But thanks be to God, which*

*giveth us the **victory through our Lord Jesus Christ.** Therefore, my beloved brethren, be ye stedfast, unmoveable, always abounding in the work of the Lord, forasmuch as ye know that **your labour is not in vain in the Lord.**"* — *1 Cor 15:50-58*

Flesh and blood cannot inherit the kingdom of God, heaven. After Jesus' resurrection he appeared to His disciples and said touch me, for I am flesh and bone. Jesus shed His blood at the cross. Glorified bodies will have no blood.

In an instant the dead will be raised, and the living will be changed. For believers, death and the grave are no longer an issue and have no power. Our victory over death and the grave is through our Lord Jesus Christ. Since Jesus was resurrected and all believers that sleep in Christ will be resurrected, know for a certainty that your labor in the gospel is not in vain.

The resurrection of the dead was no mystery as is obvious from the text. The mystery was that all believers living, and dead would be changed in a moment at an event we call the rapture of the Church. This event is a new revelation. Therefore, it is a separate and distinct event in the overall resurrection of the just. The Rapture pertains only to the Church. Martyred Tribulation saints will be raised at the end of the 7-year tribulation.

*"And I saw thrones, and they sat upon them, and judgment was given unto them: and I saw the **souls of them that were beheaded for the witness of Jesus, and for the word of God, and which had not worshipped the beast, neither his image, neither had received his mark upon their foreheads, or in their hands**; and they lived and reigned with Christ a thousand years. But the rest of the dead lived not again until the thousand years were finished. **This is the first resurrection.**"* — *Rev 20:4-5*

The phrase "This is the first resurrection" has confused many a prophecy student and teacher. Some think that this resurrection which occurs at the second coming of Jesus Christ must be the rapture because it is the first resurrection. Acts 2:15 states *"And have hope toward God, which they themselves also allow, that there shall be a resurrection of the dead, both of the just and unjust."* There are two general resurrections in the Bible, a resurrection of the just (righteous) and a resurrection of the unjust (unrighteous).

"But now is Christ risen from the dead, and become the firstfruits of them that slept." — 1 Cor 15:20

The first resurrection is the resurrections of the just, the righteous, including tribulation saints, those that die for Christ during the 7-year tribulation. That happens after the second coming of Jesus Christ. That is exactly what is happening in Rev 20 verses 4-5 previously quoted. The context of the resurrection of the just, the first resurrection, are those from Adam to the second coming of Christ.

Part Nine

The Prophetic Feasts of the Lord

Chapter Seventeen

Leviticus Chapter Twenty Three

*"And the LORD spake unto Moses, saying, Speak unto the children of Israel, and say unto them, Concerning the **feasts** of the LORD, which ye shall proclaim to be holy **convocations**, even these are my feasts." — Leviticus 23:1-2*

What is a feast? In Strong's (H4150 - "mowed") the word for feast means an appointed time, sign, or meeting.

What is a convocation; a sacred assembly, gathering, meeting and a rehearsal.

*"Six days shall work be done: but the seventh day is the sabbath of rest, an holy convocation; ye shall do no work therein: it is the sabbath of the LORD in all your dwellings. These are the **feasts** of the LORD, even holy convocations, which ye shall proclaim in their **seasons**." — Leviticus 23:3-4*

The Feasts of the Lord are meetings, signs and dress rehearsals of appointed times and seasons. Each feast has a historical and a prophetic significance.

The Spring Feasts:

*"In the **fourteenth day of the first month** at even is the **LORD'S passover**. And on the **fifteenth day of the same month** is the **feast of unleavened bread** unto the LORD: **seven days ye must eat unleavened bread**. In the first day ye shall have an holy convocation: ye shall do no servile work therein. But ye shall offer an offering made by fire unto the LORD seven days: in the seventh day is an holy convocation: ye shall do no servile work therein." — Leviticus 23:5-8*

The Feast of Passover on Nissan 14 commemorates the Passover in Egypt where the death angel passed over those homes having the blood of the lamb on the door post and lintels.

The Feast of Unleavened Bread is from Nissan 15 through the 21st and memorializes the speedy exit from Egypt; so quick there was no time to add leaven to the bread and wait for it to rise before baking.

*"And the LORD spake unto Moses, saying, Speak unto the children of Israel, and say unto them, When ye be come into the land which I give unto you, and shall reap the harvest thereof, then ye shall bring a sheaf of the **firstfruits of your harvest unto the priest**: And he shall wave the sheaf before the LORD, to be accepted for you: on the **morrow after the sabbath** the priest shall wave it." — Leviticus 23:9-10*

Firstfruits Feast is on the Sunday after the Sabbath after Passover. This occurs at the beginning of the barley harvest. The first sheath of the harvest is taken to the priest and he waves it before the Lord so the Lord will bless the harvest.

*"And ye shall count unto you from the **morrow after the sabbath**, from the day that ye brought the sheaf of the wave offering; **seven sabbaths shall be complete**: Even unto the morrow after the seventh*

*sabbath shall ye number **fifty days**; and ye shall offer a **new meat offering** unto the LORD."* — *Leviticus 23:15-16*

This is the feast of Pentecost, 50 days after the feast of Firstfruits. As the feast of Firstfruits pertains to the barley harvest, Pentecost is at the time of the wheat harvest. Pentecost also memorializes the giving of the Law to Moses at Mount Sinai.

Prophetic fulfillment of the Spring Feasts

Passover:

*"And the LORD spake unto Moses and Aaron in the **land of Egypt**, saying, This month shall be unto you the beginning of months: it shall be the first month of the year to you. Speak ye unto all the congregation of Israel, saying, In the **tenth day of this month they shall take to them every man a lamb**, according to the house of their fathers, a lamb for an house: And if the household be too little for the lamb, let him and his neighbour next unto his house take it according to the number of the souls; every man according to his eating shall make your count for the lamb. Your **lamb shall be without blemish**, a male of the first year: ye shall take it out from the sheep, or from the goats: And ye shall **keep it up until the fourteenth day** of the same month: and the whole assembly of the congregation of Israel shall kill it in the evening. And they shall take of the blood, and strike it on the two side posts and on the upper door post of the houses, wherein they shall eat it. And they shall eat the flesh in that night, roast with fire, and unleavened bread; and with bitter herbs they shall eat it. Eat not of it raw, nor sodden at all with water, but roast with fire; his head with his legs, and with the purtenance thereof. And ye shall let nothing of it remain until the morning; and that which remaineth of it until the morning ye shall burn with fire. And thus shall ye eat it;*

*with your loins girded, your shoes on your feet, and your staff in your hand; and **ye shall eat it in haste**: it is the LORD'S passover."* — *Exodus 12:1-11*

Passover lamb is selected and presented to the family on the 10th day of Nissan. Jesus rode into Jerusalem on the 10th of Nissan presenting Himself as the Lamb of God. Four days later on the fourteenth of Nissan the original Passover lamb was killed, and its blood struck on the door posts and lintel. Then the lamb is roasted whole and eaten. Jesus was crucified on Nissan 14 as the perfect Lamb without spot or blemish. Neither Herod nor Pilate found any fault in Jesus. His blood satisfied the justice of God as a propitiation for sin. Those that apply the Blood of Christ to their life pass from death unto life.

The annual Passover feast was a dress rehearsal for the appointed time of the fulfillment of the feast. Jesus said that He came not to destroy the Law but to fulfill it. Jesus fulfilled Passover to the letter by His own sacrificial blood.

Unleavened Bread:

*"And on the fifteenth day of the same month is the feast of unleavened bread unto the LORD: **seven days** ye must eat unleavened bread."* — *Leviticus 23:6*

The feast of Unleavened Bread occurs in the 7 days immediately following the Passover Feast. Leaven is a type for sin. During this 7-day period the sinless Lamb of God died, was resurrected and ascended into Heaven to present Himself before the Father as the perfect sacrificial atonement for sin and the complete satisfaction of the justice of God.

"Who being the brightness of his glory, and the express image of his person, and upholding all things by the word of his power, when he

had *by himself purged our sins, sat down on the right hand of the Majesty on high;"* — *Hebrews 1:3*

"But this man, after **he had offered one sacrifice for sins forever, sat down on the right hand of God;** *From henceforth expecting till his enemies be made his footstool. For by one offering he hath perfected forever them that are sanctified." — Hebrews 10:12-14*

Firstfruits:

"Speak unto the children of Israel, and say unto them, When ye be come into the land which I give unto you, and shall reap the harvest thereof, then ye shall bring a sheaf of the **firstfruits of your harvest** *unto the priest: And he shall wave the sheaf before the LORD, to be accepted for you: on the morrow after the sabbath the priest shall wave it." — Leviticus 23:10-11*

But now is Christ risen from the dead, and become the **firstfruits** *of them that slept. — 1 Cor 15:20*

The firstfruits speak of the resurrection of Jesus from the dead; He is the firstfruits of many that will follow at His second coming (the first resurrection). No one was resurrected with a glorified body prior to Jesus' resurrection.

Pentecost:

"And ye shall count unto you from the morrow after the sabbath, from the day that ye brought the sheaf of the wave offering; seven sabbaths shall be complete: Even unto the morrow after the seventh sabbath shall ye number **fifty days;** *and ye shall offer a new meat offering unto the LORD." — Leviticus 23:15-16*

Pentecost is at the beginning of the wheat harvest.

*"And when the day of Pentecost was fully come, they were all with one accord in one place. And suddenly there came a sound from heaven as of a rushing mighty wind, and it filled all the house where they were sitting. And there appeared unto them cloven tongues like as of fire, and it sat upon each of them. And **they were all filled with the Holy Ghost**, and began to speak with other tongues, as the Spirit gave them utterance…"* — *Acts 2:1-4*

The ancient Jewish Spring Feasts (Passover, Unleavened Bread, First-fruits, and Pentecost) were dress rehearsals for the Messiah's sacrificial death, burial, resurrection and the coming of the Holy Spirit.

The Fall Feasts:

*"And the LORD spake unto Moses, saying, Speak unto the children of Israel, saying, In the **seventh month, in the first day of the month, shall ye have a sabbath, a memorial of blowing of trumpets,** an holy convocation. Ye shall do no servile work therein: but ye shall offer an offering made by fire unto the LORD. And the LORD spake unto Moses, saying, Also on the **tenth day of this seventh month there shall be a day of atonement**: it shall be an holy convocation unto you; and ye shall afflict your souls, and offer an offering made by fire unto the LORD."* — *Leviticus 23:23-27*

*"And the LORD spake unto Moses, saying, Speak unto the children of Israel, saying, The **fifteenth day of this seventh month shall be the feast of tabernacles** for seven days unto the LORD. On the first day shall be an holy convocation: ye shall do no servile work therein. Seven days ye shall offer an offering made by fire unto the LORD: on the **eighth day shall be an holy convocation unto you; and ye shall offer an offering made by fire unto the LORD: it is a solemn***

assembly; and ye shall do no servile work therein.” — *Leviticus 23:33–36*

The Feast of Trumpets:

The Feast of Trumpets on Tishri 1 (late September) is a memorial feast for the blowing of the trumpets in the desert calling the congregation of Israel to move and also the blowing of the trumpets prior to going to war. Remember, a feast is an appointed time. It is also the beginning of the secular year, Rosh Hashanah.

*“**Blow ye the trumpet in Zion, and sound an alarm** in my holy mountain: let all the inhabitants of the land tremble: for the day of the LORD cometh, for it is nigh at hand;”* — *Joel 2:1*

*“And the LORD shall be seen over them, and his arrow shall go forth as the lightning: and the **Lord GOD shall blow the trumpet**, and shall go with whirlwinds of the south.”* — *Zechariah 9:14*

*“**Blow up the trumpet in the new moon**, in the time appointed, on our solemn feast day.”* — *Psalm 81:3*

*“If when he seeth the sword come upon the land, he **blow the trumpet, and warn the people;”* — *Ezekiel 33:3*

The future blowing of this trumpet might begin the time of Jacob's Trouble – the 7-year Tribulation

“Ask ye now, and see whether a man doth travail with child? wherefore do I see every man with his hands on his loins, as a woman in travail, and all faces are turned into paleness? Alas! for that day is

*great, so that none is like it: it is even **the time of Jacob's trouble**; but he shall be saved out of it."* — *Jeremiah 30:6-7*

The Day of Atonement:

*"Also on the tenth day of this seventh month there shall be a **day of atonement**: it shall be an holy convocation unto you; and ye shall afflict your souls, and offer an offering made by fire unto the LORD."* — *Leviticus 23:27*

*"And Aaron shall make an **atonement** upon the horns of it **once in a year with the blood of the sin offering of atonements:** once in the year shall he make atonement upon it throughout your generations: it is most holy unto the LORD."* — *Exodus 30:10*

*"But Christ being come an **high priest** of good things to come, by a greater and **more perfect tabernacle**, not made with hands, that is to say, not of this building; Neither by the blood of goats and calves, but **by his own blood he entered in once into the holy place**, having obtained eternal redemption for us. For if the blood of bulls and of goats, and the ashes of an heifer sprinkling the unclean, sanctifieth to the purifying of the flesh: How much more shall the **blood of Christ**, who through the eternal Spirit offered himself without spot to God, **purge your conscience from dead works to serve the living God?"** — *Hebrews 9:11-14*

Importance of the Blood:

o New Testament — "For this is my blood of the new testament, which is shed for many for the remission of sins." Matthew 26:28. "Likewise also the cup after supper, saying, this cup is the new testament in my blood, which is shed for you." Luke 22:20

144

- Eternal Life —"Whoso eateth my flesh, and drinketh my blood, hath eternal life; and I will raise him up at the last day." John 6:54
- Redemption — "In whom we have redemption through his blood, the forgiveness of sins, according to the riches of his grace;" Ephesians 1:7 Forasmuch as ye know that ye were not redeemed with corruptible things, as silver and gold, from your vain conversation received by tradition from your fathers; But with the precious blood of Christ, as of a lamb without blemish and without spot:" 1 Peter 1:18-19
- Atonement — "Whom God hath set forth to be a propitiation through faith in his blood, to declare his righteousness for the remission of sins that are past, through the forbearance of God;" Romans 3:25 "But if we walk in the light, as he is in the light, we have fellowship one with another, and the blood of Jesus Christ his Son cleanseth us from all sin." 1 John 1:7
- Justification — "Much more then, being now justified by his blood, we shall be saved from wrath through him." Romans 5:9
- Forgiveness and Cleansing — "In whom we have redemption through his blood, even the forgiveness of sins:" Colossians 1:14 "If we confess our sins, he is faithful and just to forgive us our sins, and to cleanse us from all unrighteousness." 1 John 1:9
- Reconciliation — "And, having made peace through the blood of his cross, by him to reconcile all things unto himself; by him, I say, whether they be things in earth, or things in heaven." Colossians 1:20
- Overcome — "And they overcame him by the blood of the Lamb and by the word of their testimony; and they loved not their lives unto the death." Revelation 12:11
- Purchased — "Take heed therefore unto yourselves, and to all the flock, over the which the Holy Ghost hath made you overseers, to feed the church of God, which he hath purchased with his own blood." Acts 20:28

*"For I would not, brethren, that ye should be ignorant of this mystery, lest ye should be wise in your own conceits; that blindness in part is happened to Israel, until the fulness of the Gentiles be come in. And so **all Israel shall be saved**: as it is written, There shall come out of Sion the Deliverer, and shall turn away ungodliness from Jacob: For this is my covenant unto them, **when I shall take away their sins**."* — Romans 11:25-27*

Messiah returns as King of Kings and Lord of Lords:

*"**Yet have I set my king upon my holy hill of Zion**. I will declare the decree: the LORD hath said unto me, Thou art my Son; this day have I begotten thee. Ask of me, and I shall give thee the heathen for thine inheritance, and the uttermost parts of the earth for thy possession."* — Psalm 2:6-8*

*"And the seventh angel sounded; and there were great voices in heaven, saying, **The kingdoms of this world are become the kingdoms of our Lord, and of his Christ; and he shall reign for ever and ever**."* — Rev 11:15*

*"And of the angels he saith, Who maketh his angels spirits, and his ministers a flame of fire. But unto the Son he saith, **Thy throne, O God, is for ever and ever: a sceptre of righteousness is the sceptre of thy kingdom**."* — Hebrews 1:7-8*

*"And he hath on his vesture and on his thigh a name written, **KING OF KINGS, AND LORD OF LORDS**."* — Revelation 19:16*

The Day of Atonement prophetically speaks of the Second Coming of Christ when He will save the remnant of Israel.

The Feast of Tabernacles:

"Speak unto the children of Israel, saying, The fifteenth day of this seventh month shall be the feast of tabernacles for seven days unto the LORD." — *Leviticus 23:34*

"And ye shall keep it a feast unto the LORD **seven days in the year**. *It shall be a statute forever in your generations: ye shall celebrate it in the seventh month.* **Ye shall dwell in booths seven days;** *all that are Israelites born shall dwell in booths: That your generations may know that I made the children of Israel to dwell in booths, when I brought them out of the land of Egypt: I am the LORD your God."* — *Leviticus 23:41-43*

"And I heard a great voice out of heaven saying, Behold, **the tabernacle of God is with men**, *and he will dwell with them, and they shall be his people, and God himself shall be with them, and be their God."* — *Rev 21:3*

"And after six days Jesus taketh with him Peter, and James, and John, and leadeth them up into an high mountain apart by themselves: and he was transfigured before them. And his raiment became shining, exceeding white as snow; so as no fuller on earth can white them. And there appeared unto them Elias with Moses: and they were talking with Jesus. And Peter answered and said to Jesus, Master, it is good for us to be here: and **let us make three tabernacles; one for thee, and one for Moses, and one for Elias.**" — *Mark 9:2-5*

The Feast of Tabernacles lasted 7 days with the last day the great day of the feast. On the 7th day the Jews would sing a song from Isaiah 12:2-3 "Behold, God is my salvation; I will trust, and not be afraid: for the LORD JEHOVAH is my

147

strength and my song; he also is become my salvation. Therefore, with joy shall ye draw water out of the wells of salvation."

John chapter 7 states *"Now the Jew's feast of tabernacles was at hand. Now about the midst of the feast Jesus went up to the temple and taught. In the last day, that great day of the feast, Jesus stood and cried, saying, If any man thirst, let him come to me and drink. He that believeth on me, as the scripture hath said, out of his belly shall flow rivers of living water."*

The prophetic fulfillment of the Feast of Tabernacles is the Millennial Reign of Christ when God will tabernacle with man.

The Feasts of the Lord:

Passover	Nissan 14 - Spring	Jesus Christ the Passover Lamb of God reconciled the world to God by His blood.
Unleavened Bread	Nissan 15-21 Spring	The sinless Lamb of God was buried.
Firstfruits	Nissan 16 - Spring	Resurrection of Jesus Christ.
Weeks	50 days after Firstfruits - Spring	The coming of the Holy Spirit.
Trumpets	Tishri 1 - Fall	Warning and alarm
Yom Kippur	Tishri 10 - Fall	Salvation of the Jews and others at the Second Coming of Jesus.
Tabernacles	Tishri 15 - Fall	God tabernacles with man in the Kingdom on earth.

Spring Feasts – Jesus' 1ˢᵗ coming – Fulfilled.

Church Age - Holy Spirit – Now.

Fall Feasts – Jesus' 2ⁿᵈ coming – Future.

*"Come, and **let us return unto the LORD**: for he hath torn, and he will heal us; he hath smitten, and he will bind us up. **After two days will he revive us: in the third day he will raise us up, and we shall live in his sight.**"* — *Hosea 6:1-2*

The Lord has torn and smitten us (Jews), but He will heal us and bind us up. After two days (two thousand years) he will revive us and in the third day (thousand-year millennial reign) He will raise us up and we will live with him.

*"But, beloved, be not ignorant of this one thing, that **one day is with the Lord as a thousand years, and a thousand years as one day.**"* — *2 Peter 3:8*

Pärt Tën

Thë Bäök äf Rëvëlätiän

Chäptër Ëïghtëën

Thë Rëvëlätiän äf Jësus Christ

*"**The Revelation of Jesus Christ**, which God gave unto him, to shew unto his servants things which **must shortly come to pass**; and he sent and signified it by his angel unto his servant John: Who bare record of the word of God, and of the testimony of Jesus Christ, and of all things that he saw. **Blessed is he** that readeth, and they that hear the words of this prophecy, and keep those things which are written therein: **for the time is at hand**." — Rev 1:1-3*

*"Surely the Lord GOD will do nothing, but **he revealeth his secret unto his servants the prophets**." — Amos 3:7*

"The secret of the LORD is with them that fear him; and he will shew them his covenant." — Psalm 25:14

*"Henceforth I call you not servants; for the servant knoweth not what his lord doeth: but **I have called you friends; for all things that I have heard of my Father I have made known unto you**." — John 15:15*

- The Book is the revelation or unveiling of Jesus Christ; the Second Coming of Christ. This is the unveiling of the glorified King of Kings ruler of heaven and earth, not the suffering servant.
- The events in the Book must shortly some to pass. We have been living in this present dispensation of grace for the past 2000 years. Why has this prophecy not "come to pass"?
- The reader of the Book is promised a blessing if he keeps the things written therein. Only those living during the time of the book can keep the book and receive the blessing.
- The time is at hand; more so today than ever.

*"John to the **seven churches which are in Asia**: Grace be unto you, and peace, from **him which is, and which was, and which is to come**; and from the seven Spirits which are before his throne; And from Jesus Christ, who is the faithful witness, and the **first begotten of the dead**, and the prince of the kings of the earth. Unto him that loved us, and washed us from our sins in his own blood, And **hath made us kings and priests unto God and his Father**; to him be glory and dominion for ever and ever. Amen."* — *Rev 1:4-6*

- Greeting from John to the seven churches; grace and peace.
- Him which is, and was, and is to come – Jesus Christ.
- First begotten of the dead – first resurrected to glorified body, Jesus Christ.
- Jewish believers will be made kings and priests unto God by Christ's blood at the second coming.

*"Behold, **he cometh with clouds**; and **every eye shall see him**, and they also **which pierced him**: and all kindreds of the earth shall wail because of him. Even so, Amen. I am Alpha and Omega, the beginning and the ending, saith the Lord, **which is, and which was, and which is to come, the Almighty**."* — *Rev 1:7-8*

*"**Clouds** and darkness are round about him: righteousness and judgment are the habitation of his throne."* — Psalm 97:2

*"The burden of Egypt. Behold, the LORD **rideth upon a swift cloud,** and shall come into Egypt:"* — Isaiah 19:1

*"I saw in the night visions, and, behold, one like the **Son of man came with the clouds** of heaven, and came to the Ancient of days, and they brought him near before him."* — Dan 7:13

*"And then shall appear the sign of the Son of man in heaven: and then shall all the tribes of the earth mourn, and they shall see the Son of man **coming in the clouds of heaven** with power and great glory."* — Mat 24:30

*"Ascribe ye strength unto God: his excellency is over Israel, and **his strength is in the clouds.**"* — Psalm 68:34

- o When Jesus returns, he will come in the clouds. In Acts Jesus was received up into the clouds so likewise he will appear.
- o When Jesus appears, the Jews will see the Son that they pierced (on the cross).
- o Again, Jesus is, was, and is to come, the Almighty.

*"I John, who also am your brother, and companion in tribulation, and in the kingdom and patience of Jesus Christ, was in the **isle that is called Patmos,** for the word of God, and for the testimony of Jesus Christ. **I was in the Spirit on the Lord's day,** and heard behind me a **great voice, as of a trumpet,** Saying, **I am Alpha and Omega, the first and the last:** and, What thou seest, **write in a book,** and **send it unto the seven churches which are in Asia;** unto Ephesus, and unto Smyrna, and unto Pergamos, and unto Thyatira, and unto Sardis, and unto Philadelphia, and unto Laodicea."* — Rev 1:9-11

- o John was on the island of Patmos off the coast of Turkey.
- o He was in the Spirit on the Lord's Day (Day of the Lord) and heard a voice as the sound of a trumpet. "And it came to pass on the third day in the morning, that there were thunders and lightnings, and a **thick cloud** upon the mount, and the **voice of the trumpet exceeding loud;** so that all the people that was in the camp trembled." - Exodus 19:16. God's voice is as a trumpet.
- o The Lord identifies Himself as the Alpha and Omega, the beginning and the last. "Who hath wrought and done it, calling the generations **from the beginning**? I the LORD, **the first, and with the last;** I am he." — Isaiah 41:4
- o John commanded to write what he sees in a book and distribute to the seven churches in Asia Minor.

"Now go, write it before them in a table, and note it in a book, that it may be for the time to come for ever and ever:" — Isaiah 30:8

"Thus speaketh the LORD God of Israel, saying, Write thee all the words that I have spoken unto thee in a book." — Jeremiah 30:2

*"And I turned to see the voice that spake with me. And being turned, I saw **seven golden candlesticks;** And in the midst of the seven candlesticks one like unto the **Son of man**, clothed with a garment down to the foot, and girt about the paps with a **golden girdle**. His head and his hairs were **white like wool**, as white as snow; and his eyes were as **a flame of fire;** And **his feet like unto fine brass**, as if they burned in a furnace; and his voice as the **sound of many waters**. And he had in his right hand seven stars: and out of his mouth went a sharp twoedged sword: and his countenance was as the sun shineth in his strength. I am he that **liveth, and was dead; and, behold, I am alive for evermore,** Amen; and have the keys of hell and of death." — Rev 1:12-18*

*"I beheld till the thrones were cast down, and the Ancient of days did sit, whose **garment was white as snow, and the hair of his head like the pure wool:** his throne was like the **fiery flame,** and his wheels as burning fire. **A fiery stream issued and came forth from before him:** thousand thousands ministered unto him, and ten thousand times ten thousand stood before him: the judgment was set, and the books were opened."* — Daniel 7:9-10

*"Then I lifted up mine eyes, and looked, and behold a certain man **clothed in linen,** whose loins were girded with **fine gold of Uphaz:** His body also was like the beryl, and his face as the appearance of lightning, and **his eyes as lamps of fire,** and his arms and his feet like in **colour to polished brass,** and the voice of his words like the **voice of a multitude**."* — Daniel 10:5-6

The text of Revelation above is almost a direct quote from Daniel chapters 7 and 10. The text in Daniel pertains directly to the Day of the Lord, the Second Coming of Christ.

A flame of fire:

- o *"But who may abide the day of his coming? and who shall stand when he appeareth? for **he is like a refiner's fire**"* — *Malachi 3:2*
- o *"Neither their silver nor their gold shall be able to deliver them in the day of the LORD'S wrath; but the **whole land shall be devoured by the fire of his jealousy:** for he shall make even a speedy riddance of all them that dwell in the land."* — Zephaniah 1:18
- o *"A **fire goeth before him,** and burneth up his enemies round about."* — Psalm 97:3

- *"And they shall know that I am the LORD, when I have **set a fire in Egypt**, and when all her helpers shall be destroyed." — Ezekiel 30:8*
- *"But I will **send a fire into the house of Hazael**, which shall devour the palaces of Benhadad." — Amos 1:4*
- *"But I will **send a fire on the wall of Gaza**, which shall devour the palaces thereof." — Amos 1:7*
- *"But I will **send a fire on the wall of Tyrus**, which shall devour the palaces thereof." — Amos 1:10*
- *'But I will **send a fire upon Teman**, which shall devour the palaces of Bozrah." — Amos 1:12*

*"**Write the things which thou hast seen**, and the **things which are**, and the **things which shall be hereafter;** The mystery of the seven stars which thou sawest in my right hand, and the seven golden candlesticks. The **seven stars are the angels of the seven churches**: and the **seven candlesticks which thou sawest are the seven churches**." — Rev 1:19-20*

There are three categories of writings in the Book. The Lord Jesus gives the outline for the entire Book of Revelation.
1. Things that John has seen (Chapter 1).
2. Things which are in the Day of the Lord, Chapters 2 & 3).
3. Things that shall come during the Day of the Lord (Chapters 4 - 22).

The seven candlesticks are the seven churches. The seven stars are the angels of the seven churches.

Chapter Nineteen
The Letters to the Churches

Church of Ephesus

*"Unto the angel of the **church of Ephesus** write; These things saith he that holdeth the seven stars in his right hand, who walketh in the midst of the seven golden candlesticks; **I know thy works, and thy labour, and thy patience, and how thou canst not bear them which are evil:** and thou hast tried them which say they are apostles, and are not, and hast found them liars: And hast borne, and hast patience, and for **my name's sake hast laboured, and hast not fainted. Nevertheless I have somewhat against thee, because thou hast left thy first love.** Remember therefore from whence thou art fallen, and **repent**, and do the first works; or else I will come unto thee quickly, and will remove thy candlestick out of his place, except thou repent. But this thou hast, that thou **hatest the deeds of the Nicolaitans**, which I also hate. He that hath an ear, let him hear what the Spirit saith unto the churches; To him that overcometh will I give to eat of the tree of life, which is in the midst of the paradise of God." — Rev 2:1-7*

Remember, John is in the Spirit during the future Day of the Lord. These seven churches will exist during the Tribulation. They are not Pauline grace churches of the 1st century. They are not modern-day Christian churches either. They are assemblies of Jews during the Tribulation.

The church of Ephesus, located in western Asia Minor with the other six, was doing well in church activities but seem to have little time for the King. They had left their first love by not

157

spending devotional time with Christ. They were patient in their labors and did not tolerate false teachers. However, they needed to repent of slipping away from Jesus Christ. Those that repent and overcome will eat from the tree of life in the Millennial Kingdom.

Nicolaitans – followers of the Greek heretic Nicholas who desires to establish a clerical hierarchy over the laity. These folks were hated and not allowed to establish a hierarchy to rule over the church.

Church in Smyrna

*"And unto the angel of the **church in Smyrna** write; These things saith the first and the last, which was dead, and is alive; **I know thy works, and tribulation, and poverty, (but thou art rich)** and I know the **blasphemy of them which say they are Jews, and are not, but are the synagogue of Satan.** Fear none of those things which thou shalt suffer: behold, the devil shall cast some of you into prison, that ye may be tried; and ye shall have tribulation ten days: **be thou faithful unto death**, and I will give thee a **crown of life**. He that hath an ear, let him hear what the Spirit saith unto the churches; He that overcometh shall **not be hurt of the second death.**" — Rev 2:8-11*

The church in Smyrna will suffer greatly under Antichrist persecution. Their poverty will be great because the beast will confiscate the property of Jews, but the Lord said they are rich; rich in the power of the Lord not in the things of this world. This is a sharp contrast to the folks at Laodicea who boasted about being rich but were actually poor, miserable, blind, wretched and naked.

Smyrna is the martyred church, and the root of the name is myrrh which means death. The believers are told to be faithful unto death and they will receive the martyr's crown, the crown of life.

Church in Pergamos

*"And to the angel of the **church in Pergamos** write; These things saith he which hath the sharp sword with two edges; I know thy works, and where thou **dwellest, even where Satan's seat is:** and **thou holdest fast my name**, and **hast not denied my faith**, even in those days wherein Antipas was my faithful martyr, who was slain among you, where Satan dwelleth. **But I have a few things against thee,** because thou hast there them that hold the **doctrine of Balaam**, who taught Balac to cast a stumblingblock before the children of Israel, to eat things sacrificed unto idols, and to commit fornication. So hast thou also them that hold **the doctrine of the Nicolaitans**, which thing I hate. **Repent; or else I will come unto thee quickly, and will fight against them with the sword of my mouth.** He that hath an ear, let him hear what the Spirit saith unto the churches; To him that overcometh will I give to eat of the hidden manna, and will give him a white stone, and in the stone a new name written, which no man knoweth saving he that receiveth it."* — Rev 2:12-17

Satan's seat was moved from Babylon to Pergamos after the Persians invaded Babylon in the 6th century B.C. The future believers are holding fast and not denying the Lord but have allowed some false teachers into the body. There are some there that teach the doctrine of Balaam allowing idols and fornication. The Balaam teachers are also in it for gain; they make merchandise of the saints and are always looking for ways to make money from the gospel. Nothing much has changed; there are plenty of those types around today.

Church in Thyatira

*"And unto the angel of the **church in Thyatira** write; These things saith the Son of God, who hath his eyes like unto a flame of fire, and*

159

his feet are like fine brass; **I know thy works, and charity, and service, and faith, and thy patience, and thy works; and the last to be more than the first.** *Notwithstanding I have a few things against thee, because thou sufferest that woman* **Jezebel,** *which calleth herself a prophetess,* **to teach and to seduce my servants to commit fornication, and to eat things sacrificed unto idols.** *And I gave her space to repent of her fornication; and she repented not. Behold, I will cast her into a bed, and them that commit adultery with her* **into great tribulation,** *except they repent of their deeds. And I will kill her children with death; and all the churches shall know that I am he which searcheth the reins and hearts: and I will give unto every one of you according to your works. But unto you I say, and unto the rest in Thyatira, as many as have not this doctrine, and which have not known the depths of Satan, as they speak; I will put upon you none other burden. But that which ye have already* **hold fast till I come.** *And he that overcometh, and keepeth my works unto the end, to him will I give* **power over the nations:** *And he shall* **rule them with a rod of iron;** *as the vessels of a potter shall they be broken to shivers: even as I received of my Father. And I will give him the morning star. He that hath an ear, let him hear what the Spirit saith unto the churches."* — Rev 2:18-29

The church in Thyatira will improve in their service to the Lord but for some reason tolerate a woman named Jezebel. Like the teachers of Balaam, she brings in idols and fornication to pollute the Jews just as the Jezebel of old. But there is a group that will not follow her pernicious ways and will hold fast to the truth. The Lord instructs them to "hold fast till I come." This is the first reference to the coming of the Lord in the seven letters. This tells us that the church of Thyatira is a church that will exist in the last days. The group that follows Jezebel are told they will be cast into the great tribulation, the last half of the 7-year

Tribulation. The implication is that the true believers will be protected during the last 3 ½ years of the Tribulation.

Church in Sardis

*"And unto the angel of the **church in Sardis** write; These things saith he that hath the seven Spirits of God, and the seven stars; I know thy works, that **thou hast a name that thou livest, and art dead.** Be watchful, and **strengthen the things which remain**, that are ready to die: for I have not found thy works perfect before God. Remember therefore how thou hast received and heard, and **hold fast, and repent.** If therefore **thou shalt not watch, I will come on thee as a thief, and thou shalt not know what hour I will come upon thee.** Thou hast a few names even in Sardis which have not defiled their garments; and they shall walk with me in white: for they are worthy. He that overcometh, the same shall be clothed in white raiment; and I will not blot out his name out of the book of life, but I will confess his name before my Father, and before his angels. He that hath an ear, let him hear what the Spirit saith unto the churches."*
— Rev 3:1-6

This church has a name, a reputation, but is spiritually dead; not sick or ill, but dead. They are told to strengthen those few things that remain before they die also. It they do not repent the Lord will come upon them "as a thief." This is a reference to the second coming of the Lord as a thief to those that are not watching for Him. The believers are commended to watch for the coming of the Lord and be ready. The overcomers will be clothed in white raiment which is symbolic of the righteousness of Jesus Christ.

Church in Philadelphia

*"And to the angel of the **church in Philadelphia** write; These things saith he that is holy, he that is true, he that hath the key of David, he that openeth, and no man shutteth; and shutteth, and no man openeth; I know thy works: behold, I have **set before thee an open door,** and no man can shut it: for **thou hast a little strength, and hast kept my word, and hast not denied my name.** Behold, I will make them of the synagogue of Satan, which say they are Jews, and are not, but do lie; behold, I will make them to come and worship before thy feet, and to know that I have loved thee. Because thou **hast kept the word of my patience, I also will keep thee from the hour of temptation, which shall come upon all the world, to try them that dwell upon the earth.** Behold, I come quickly: **hold that fast which thou hast, that no man take thy crown.** Him that overcometh will I make a pillar in the temple of my God, and he shall go no more out: and I will write upon him the name of my God, and the name of the city of my God, which is new Jerusalem, which cometh down out of heaven from my God: and I will write upon him my new name. He that hath an ear, let him hear what the Spirit saith unto the churches." — Rev 3:7-13*

The churches of Philadelphia and Smyrna are the only two churches to which nothing bad is stated. They are both told to hang in there, hold fast. The Lord Jesus Christ commends the church of Philadelphia and states that He will "keep thee from the hour of temptation, which shall come upon the whole world." The word "from" in the Greek is ek and means "out of" or "away from." The meaning here is that the believers in Philadelphia will be protected from the last half of the 7-year tribulation period that will come upon the whole world. This is the remnant of Israel protected for 3 ½ years:

"And to the woman were given two wings of a great eagle, that she might fly into the wilderness, into her place, where she is nourished for a time, and times, and half a time, from the face of the serpent." - Revelation 12:14 KJV

Church of the Laodiceans

*"And unto the angel of the **church of the Laodiceans** write; These things saith the Amen, the faithful and true witness, the beginning of the creation of God; I know thy works, that **thou art neither cold nor hot: I would thou wert cold or hot. So then because thou art lukewarm, and neither cold nor hot, I will spue thee out of my mouth.** Because thou sayest, I am rich, and increased with goods, and have need of nothing; and knowest not that **thou art wretched, and miserable, and poor, and blind, and naked:** I counsel thee to buy of me gold tried in the fire, that thou mayest be rich; and white raiment, that thou mayest be clothed, and that the shame of thy nakedness do not appear; and anoint thine eyes with eyesalve, that thou mayest see. **As many as I love, I rebuke and chasten:** be zealous therefore, and **repent.** Behold, I stand at the door, and knock: if any man hear my voice, and open the door, I will come in to him, and will sup with him, and he with me. To him that overcometh will I grant to sit with me in my throne, even as I also overcame, and am set down with my Father in his throne. He that hath an ear, let him hear what the Spirit saith unto the churches."* — Rev 3:14-22

The church of Laodicea is the lukewarm church. This typifies many churches see in America today. They are rich and have need of nothing but are poor in the things of God, wretched in their pride, miserable in their self-deception, blind to the truths of the Lord and naked before God as He sees everything. They are told to repent and pursue the things of God. If they do not repent Jesus will spew them out into the

163

Great Tribulation, the last half of the 7-year Tribulation. Notice that Jesus is standing outside the church and knocking on the door. Hopefully some will invite Him in.

Summary table:

	Ephesus	Smyrna	Pergamos	Thyatira
Meaning	Let go	Anointing oil	Married to power	Ruled by a woman
Character	Relaxed	Martyrs and tribulation	Union of Church and State	Counterfeit, Anti-God
Jesus' Title	Walks in the midst of the candlesticks	Was dead and is alive	He which has the sharp sword	The Son of God
Good	Patience and Labor	Endured tribulation	Faith not denied	Faith and patience
Faults	Left their first love	NONE	Balaam's idolatry	Ruled by Jezebel
Rewards to Overcomers	Paradise	The first resurrection	A white stone	Reign with Christ

Summary table cont'd:

	Sardis	Philadelphia	Laodicea
Meaning	A precious stone	Brotherly love	Laity
Character	Apostate	Evangelical	Modernism, Post-modernism, Humanism, Universalism, etc.
Jesus' Title	He that has the Seven Spirits	Holy and true	Faithful witness
Good	A name that lived	Kept the Word	NONE
Faults	Spiritually dead	NONE	Lukewarm
Rewards to Overcomers	Name confessed before the Father	The New Jerusalem	Reign with Jesus on David's throne

Chäptër Twënty
Thë Öpën Däär

*"After this I looked, and, behold, **a door was opened in heaven**: and the first voice which I heard was as it were of **a trumpet talking with me**; which said, **Come up hither, and I will shew thee things which must be hereafter.** And **immediately** I was in the spirit: and, behold, a throne was set in heaven, and one sat on the throne. And he that sat was to look upon like a jasper and a sardine stone: and there was a rainbow round about the throne, in sight like unto an emerald. And **round about the throne were four and twenty seats**: and upon the seats I saw **four and twenty elders sitting, clothed in white raiment; and they had on their heads crowns of gold.**"* — *Rev 4:1-4*

*"Then said Jesus unto them again, Verily, verily, I say unto you, **I am the door** of the sheep."* — *John 10:7*

*"**I am the door**: by me if any man enter in, he shall be saved, and shall go in and out, and find pasture."* — *John 10:9*

From the beginning of chapter 4 thru chapter 21 the churches are not mentioned but most will experience the events contained therein. The entire Book of Revelation is remarkably Jewish.

"Come up hither" - John is taken up to heaven to witness the events of the 7-year Tribulation. This happens before the

165

tribulation begins with the opening of the first seal in chapter six.

"Things hereafter" – Chapters 4 and following are hereafter (future).

Hearing the voice of God as a trumpet, John was immediately in the spirit and in heaven. John sees a beautiful throne in heaven made of precious stones circled by an emerald rainbow. There are 24 crowned elders sitting in thrones round about the emerald throne.

*"And out of the throne proceeded lightnings and thunderings and voices: and there were **seven lamps of fire burning before the throne, which are the seven Spirits of God**. And before the throne there was a sea of glass like unto crystal: and in the midst of the throne, and round about the throne, were **four beasts** full of eyes before and behind. And the first beast was **like a lion**, and the second beast **like a calf**, and the third beast had a **face as a man**, and the fourth beast was like a **flying eagle**. And the four beasts had each of them six wings about him; and they were full of eyes within: and they rest not day and night, saying, Holy, holy, holy, Lord God Almighty, **which was, and is, and is to come**. And when those beasts give glory and honour and thanks to him that sat on the throne, who liveth for ever and ever, The **four and twenty elders fall down** before him that sat on the throne, and worship him that liveth for ever and ever, and cast their crowns before the throne, saying, **Thou art worthy**, O Lord, to receive glory and honour and power: for thou hast created all things, and for thy pleasure they are and were created." — Rev 4:5-11*

The seven lamps before God could be the seven lampstands of the seven churches.

The Design (Faces) of the Gospels:

	Matthew	Mark	Luke	John
Presents:	Messiah	Servant	Son of Man	Son of God
Genealogy:	Abraham		Adam	Eternal
Jesus	Said	Did	Felt	Was
To the:	Jew	Roman	Greek	Church
1st Miracle:	Leper cleansed	Demon exp.	Demon exp.	Water to wine
Ends with:	Resurrection	Ascension	Promise of H.S.	Promise of His return
Camp Site:	East	West	South	North
Ensign:	Judah	Ephraim	Reuben	Dan
Face:	Lion	Ox	Man	Eagle

*"As for the likeness of their faces, they four had the **face of a man**, and the **face of a lion**, on the right side: and they four had the **face of an ox** on the left side; they four also had the **face of an eagle**."* — *Ezekiel 1:10 (Read Ezekiel chapter one)*

"Above it stood the seraphims: each one had six wings; with twain he covered his face, and with twain he covered his feet, and with twain he did fly." — *Isaiah 6:2*

*"I will call upon the LORD, **who is worthy to be praised**: so shall I be saved from mine enemies."* — *Psalm 18:3*

"He is the Rock, his work is perfect: for all his ways are judgment: a God of truth and without iniquity, just and right is he." — *Deut 32:4*

*"And I saw in the right hand of him that sat on the throne a **book written within and on the backside, sealed with seven seals.** And I saw a strong angel proclaiming with a loud voice, **Who is worthy to open the book, and to loose the seals thereof?** And no man in heaven, nor in earth, neither under the earth, was able to open the book, neither to look thereon. **And I wept much, because no man was found worthy to open and to read the book, neither to look thereon.**"* — Rev 5:1-4

*"And when I looked, behold, an hand was sent unto me; and, lo, a **roll of a book** was therein; And he spread it before me; and it was written within and without: and there was written therein lamentations, and mourning, and woe."* — Ezekiel 2:9-10

"And the vision of all is become unto you as the words of a book that is sealed, which men deliver to one that is learned, saying, Read this, I pray thee: and he saith, I cannot; for it is sealed:" — Isaiah 29:11

"Who hath directed the Spirit of the LORD, or being his counsellor hath taught him?" — Isaiah 40:13

"For who hath known the mind of the Lord? or who hath been his counsellor?" — Rom 11:34

The sealed book is the title deed to the earth and each seal will bring a judgment upon the earth. The time of Satan's dominion on earth is drawing to a close and Jesus is about to reclaim the earth by breaking the seals and opening the book. This is the most important escrow closing in the history of the universe. Man's six-thousand-year lease is up. The book is a scroll with writing on the outside. John knows exactly what the scroll is because he reacts dramatically when no one is found that can open the seals.

"And one of the elders saith unto me, **Weep not: behold, the Lion of the tribe of Juda, the Root of David, hath prevailed to open the book, and to loose the seven seals thereof.** *And I beheld, and, lo, in the midst of the throne and of the four beasts, and in the midst of the elders,* **stood a Lamb** *as it had been slain, having seven horns and seven eyes, which are the seven Spirits of God sent forth into all the earth. And he came and took the book out of the right hand of him that sat upon the throne. And when he had taken the book, the four beasts and* **four and twenty elders fell down before the Lamb,** *having every one of them harps, and golden vials full of odours, which are the prayers of saints. And they sung a new song, saying,* **Thou art worthy to take the book, and to open the seals thereof: for thou wast slain, and hast redeemed us to God by thy blood out of every kindred, and tongue, and people, and nation; And hast made us unto our God kings and priests: and we shall reign on the earth."** *— Rev 5:5-10*

"The **sceptre shall not depart from Judah,** *nor a lawgiver from between his feet,* **until Shiloh come;** *and unto him shall the gathering of the people be." — Genesis 49:10*

"And there shall come forth a **rod out of the stem of Jesse,** *and a Branch shall grow out of his roots:" — Isaiah 11:1*

"And **in that day there shall be a root of Jesse,** *which shall stand for an ensign of the people; to it shall the Gentiles seek: and his rest shall be glorious." — Isaiah 11:10*

"Behold, the days come, saith the LORD, that I will raise unto David a righteous Branch, and a King shall reign and prosper, and shall execute judgment and justice in the earth. In his days Judah shall be saved, and Israel shall dwell safely: and this is his name whereby he

shall be called, THE LORD OUR RIGHTEOUSNESS." —
Jeremiah 23:5-6

"Concerning his Son Jesus Christ our Lord, which was made of the
seed of David *according to the flesh;"* — *Rom 1:3*
"And again, Esaias saith, There shall be a root of Jesse, and he that
shall rise to reign over the Gentiles; in him shall the Gentiles trust."
— *Romans 15:12 (Paul quotes Isaiah 11:10)*

      Finally, the Lion of the tribe of Judah, the Root of David, the Lamb, the Lord Jesus Christ comes forth to open the book. The 24 elders fall and worship the Lord Jesus and praise Him as worthy to open the book.

      We can now possibly answer the question; who do the 24 elders represent? Notice the praise they offer:

- o Thou was slain.
- o You have redeemed us by your blood from all the world.
- o Thou has made us priests and kings.
- o We shall reign on earth.

      Since the believing Jews will rule and reign on earth with Jesus Christ, while the body of Christ rules from heaven, the 24 elders represent Israel.

      These 24 elders represent the 12 patriarchs of Israel and Jesus' 12 disciples. They are fully crowned and rewarded in heaven with Jesus before the first seal is opened. The breaking of the first seal begins the 7-year tribulation as this seal reveals the Antichrist.

"And I beheld, and I heard the voice of many angels round about the
throne and the beasts and the elders: and the number of them was ten
thousand times ten thousand, and thousands of thousands; Saying
with a loud voice, ***Worthy is the Lamb that was slain to receive***
power, and riches, and wisdom, and strength, and honour, and

*glory, **and blessing.*** *And every creature which is in heaven, and on the earth, and under the earth, and such as are in the sea, and all that are in them, heard I saying, Blessing, and honour, and glory, and power, be unto him that sitteth upon the throne, and unto the Lamb for ever and ever. And the four beasts said, Amen. And the four and twenty elders fell down and worshipped him that liveth for ever and ever." — Rev 5:11-14*

*"**A fiery stream issued and came forth from before him**: thousand thousands ministered unto him, and ten thousand times ten thousand stood before him: the judgment was set, and the books were opened." — Daniel 7:10*

"The Father loveth the Son, and hath given all things into his hand." — John 3:35

"Thine, O LORD, is the greatness, and the power, and the glory, and the victory, and the majesty: for all that is in the heaven and in the earth is thine; thine is the kingdom, O LORD, and thou art exalted as head above all." — 1 Chronicles 29:11

Notice the praise distinction in the elders and the angels. Only the elders praise the redemptive work of Christ. Jesus did not redeem angels. Only the Lamb of God is worthy to open the book.

Chäptër Twënty Önë
Thë Sëvën Sëalš

The first four seals:

*"And I saw when the **Lamb opened one of the seals**, and I heard, as it were the noise of thunder, one of the four beasts saying, Come and see. And I saw, and **behold a white horse: and he that sat on him had a bow; and a crown was given unto him: and he went forth conquering, and to conquer.** And when he had opened **the second seal**, I heard the second beast say, Come and see. And there **went out another horse that was red: and power was given to him that sat thereon to take peace from the earth, and that they should kill one another: and there was given unto him a great sword.** And when he had opened the **third seal**, I heard the third beast say, Come and see. And I beheld, and lo **a black horse; and he that sat on him had a pair of balances in his hand.** And I heard a voice in the midst of the four beasts say, A measure of wheat for a penny, and three measures of barley for a penny; and see thou hurt not the oil and the wine. And when he had opened the **fourth seal**, I heard the voice of the fourth beast say, Come and see. And I looked, and **behold a pale horse: and his name that sat on him was Death, and Hell followed with him. And power was given unto them** over the fourth part of the earth, to kill with sword, and with hunger, and with death, and with the beasts of the earth." — Rev 6:1-8*

The infamous four horsemen of the apocalypse are about to ride. Who is opening the Seals? The Lamb – Jesus; He is releasing the four horsemen upon the earth.

173

White Horse: this is none other than the Antichrist, going forth the conquer nations. He is given a bow (power) and a crown (authority). He will be a persuasive ruler and military genius. As we have seen in previous studies, he will arrive and rise to prominence on a peace platform and deceive many through flatteries.

This first seal begins the 7-year tribulation when the Antichrist confirms the 7-year peace treaty with Israel and the surrounding nations (Dan 9:27). It also begins the judgments of the wrath of God upon a Christ rejecting Israel and world (Day of the Lord).

*"Howl ye; for **the day of the LORD** is at hand; it shall come as a destruction from the Almighty." — Isaiah 13-6*

*"For it is **the day of the LORD'S vengeance**, and the year of recompences for the controversy of Zion." — Isaiah 34:8*

*"For this is **the day of the Lord GOD of hosts**, a **day of vengeance**, that he may avenge him of his adversaries: and the sword shall devour, and it shall be satiate and made drunk with their blood: for the Lord GOD of hosts hath a sacrifice in the north country by the river Euphrates." — Jeremiah 46:10*

*"For the day is near, even **the day of the LORD** is near, a cloudy day; it shall be the **time of the heathen**." — Ezekiel 30:3*

*"for the **day of the LORD** cometh, for it is nigh at hand; A **day of darkness** and of **gloominess**, a day of clouds and of **thick darkness**," — Joel 1:1-2*

*"That day is a **day of wrath, a day of trouble and distress**, a **day of wasteness** and desolation, a **day of darkness and gloominess, a day of clouds and thick darkness**," — Zephaniah 1:15*

*"And through his policy also he shall cause craft to prosper in his hand; and he shall magnify himself in his heart, and **by peace shall destroy many**: he shall also **stand up against the Prince of princes**; but he shall be broken without hand." — Daniel 8:25*

The Red Horse: This is War. Peace is taken from the earth (land) and war breaks out in the Middle East. The phrase "that they should kill one another" is interesting and may have a dual meaning. Not only do the radical Muslims want to kill Jews but they also want to kill other Muslims. Shiites want to kill Sunnis and vice versa. The rider is given a great sword meaning great wars are to come, WW3.

The Black Horse: The rider has a balance in his hand. This is symbolic of food being sold in small portions by weight implying scarcity and costliness. There will be famines in various places due to the cost and scarcity of food. However, the rich will have plenty as the "oil and wine" are guarded and handled like treasure.

The Pale Horse: After war and famine there is death. Notice that hell follows this horse. He can only take those destined for hell. The tribulation saints that are martyred immediately go to heaven as in the next verse we see them by the altar of God.

Power is given to the four horsemen over a fourth part of the earth. The Antichrist will not initially lead a one world government as some proclaim but only have power over one fourth of the earth, the Middle East. Many men and organizations have proposed and tried to implement a one world

175

order, but all have failed. There will be no one world order until Jesus inaugurates His Millennial Kingdom.

Comparison of the first 5 seals with Matthew 24:

Matthew 24	Revelation 6
v. 5 False Christ's (spirit of Antichrist)	1st Seal – White horse, Antichrist revealed
v. 6 Wars and rumors of wars	2nd Seal – Red horse – power to make war
v. 7 Famine	3rd Seal – Black horse - famine
v. 7 Pestilences, earthquakes	4th Seal – Pale horse - death
v. 9 Saints killed for His name sake	5th Seal – Martyred souls under the alter

*"And when he had opened the **fifth seal**, I saw under the altar the **souls of them that were slain for the word of God, and for the testimony which they held:** And they cried with a loud voice, saying, How long, O Lord, holy and true, dost thou not **judge and avenge our blood on them that dwell on the earth?** And white robes were given unto every one of them; and it was said unto them, that they should rest yet for a little season, until their **fellowservants also and their brethren**, that should be killed as they were, should be fulfilled."*
— *Rev 6:9-11*

Fifth Seal — Martyred Tribulation Saints:

These souls under the altar are those that have been martyred during the tribulation; they have nothing to do with the Church, the body of Christ, during this present dispensation of grace. Notice that these saints are asking the Lord for vengeance. When the church saints were being martyred they were asking for forgiveness for their enemies, not vengeance.

Two examples are the Lord himself and Steven. During the tribulation there will be many people martyred for their testimony of the Lord, mostly Jews.

In Rev 20:4 we see those beheaded for their testimony and not taking the mark of the beast meaning that through the entire 7-year period, Jewish believers are martyred for Christ. Who beheads as a form of execution? Islamic terrorist groups and nations.

*"And he shall speak great words against the most High, and **shall wear out the saints of the most High,** and think to change times and laws: and they shall be given into his hand until a time and times and the dividing of time."* — *Dan 7:25*

*"And his power shall be mighty, but not by his own power: and he shall destroy wonderfully, and shall prosper, and practise, and **shall destroy the mighty and the holy people."*** — *Dan 8:24*

*"And it was **given unto him to make war with the saints, and to overcome them:** and power was given him over all kindreds, and tongues, and nations."* — *Rev 13:7*

During the 2000-year Church Age the Church suffered under the wrath of Satan and man but NEVER the wrath of the Lord. During the 7-year tribulation the world will suffer under the terrible wrath of the Lord.

*"And I beheld when he had opened **the sixth seal,** and, lo, there was a **great earthquake;** and the **sun became black** as sackcloth of hair, and the **moon became as blood;** And the **stars of heaven fell unto the earth,** even as a fig tree casteth her untimely figs, when she is shaken of a mighty wind. And the **heaven departed as a scroll when it is rolled together; and every mountain and island were moved out of their places.** And the kings of the earth, and the great men, and the*

*rich men, and the chief captains, and the mighty men, and every bondman, and every free man, **hid themselves in the dens and in the rocks of the mountains**; And said to the mountains and rocks, Fall on us, and **hide us** from the face of him that sitteth on the throne, and **from the wrath of the Lamb: For the great day of his wrath is come**; and who shall be able to stand?"— Rev 6:12-17*

Many scholars believe that the sixth seal occurs at the middle of the 7-year tribulation and corresponds to the abomination of desolation stated in Daniel 12, Matthew 24 and 2 Thessalonians 2. But the 7th trumpet marks the mid-point of the Tribulation, not the 6th seal. At the 6th seal we see earthquakes and cosmological events in the sun, moon, and stars. The heaven departing as a scroll rolled up could refer to a nuclear exchange that causes this type of occurrence in the atmosphere.

*"The **sun shall be turned into darkness**, and the **moon into blood**, before the **great and the terrible day of the LORD come**." — Joel 2:31 (repeated by Peter in Acts 2)*

*"And all the host of heaven shall be dissolved, and **the heavens shall be rolled together as a scroll**: and all their host shall fall down, as the leaf falleth off from the vine, and **as a falling fig from the fig tree**." — Isaiah 34:4 (In reference to the destruction of Idumea and Bozrah, Jordan and western Arabia)*

*"And it waxed great, even to the host of heaven; and **it cast down some of the host and of the stars to the ground**, and stamped upon them." — Daniel 8:10*

*"And all the host of heaven shall be dissolved, and the **heavens shall be rolled together as a scroll**: and all their host shall fall down, as the*

*leaf falleth off from the vine, and as a **falling fig from the fig tree**."*
— Isaiah 34:4

*"**Enter into the rock**, and hide thee in the dust, for fear of the LORD, and for the glory of his majesty. The lofty looks of man shall be humbled, and the haughtiness of men shall be bowed down, and the **LORD alone shall be exalted in that day**. For the day of the LORD of hosts shall be upon every one that is proud and lofty, and upon every one that is lifted up; and he shall be brought low: And upon all the **cedars of Lebanon**, that are high and lifted up, and upon all the **oaks of Bashan**, And upon all the **high mountains, and upon all the hills that are lifted up**... And the loftiness of man shall be bowed down, and the haughtiness of men shall be made low: and the **LORD alone shall be exalted in that day**. And **they shall go into the holes of the rocks, and into the caves of the earth, for fear of the LORD**, and for the glory of his majesty, when he ariseth to shake terribly the earth... **To go into the clefts of the rocks**, and into the tops of the ragged rocks, for fear of the LORD, and for the glory of his majesty, when he ariseth to shake terribly the earth." — Isaiah 2:10-21*

The rulers of the surrounding nations will hide themselves in the rocks and caves trying to hide from the wrath of the lamb, the Lord Jesus Christ.

*"Behold, I am against thee, O destroying mountain, saith the LORD, which destroyest all the earth: and I will stretch out mine hand upon thee, **and roll thee down from the rocks, and will make thee a burnt mountain**." — Jeremiah 51:25*

The 144,000 thousand:

*"And after these things **I saw four angels standing on the four corners of the earth**, holding the **four winds of the earth**, that the*

179

wind should not blow on the earth, nor on the sea, nor on any tree. And I saw another angel ascending from the east, having the seal of the living God: and he cried with a loud voice to the four angels, to whom it was given to hurt the earth and the sea, Saying, **Hurt not the earth, neither the sea, nor the trees, till we have sealed the servants of our God in their foreheads**. *And I heard the number of them which were sealed: and there were sealed an* **hundred and forty and four thousand of all the tribes of the children of Israel.** *Of the tribe of Juda were sealed twelve thousand. Of the tribe of Reuben were sealed twelve thousand. Of the tribe of Gad were sealed twelve thousand. Of the tribe of Aser were sealed twelve thousand. Of the tribe of Nepthalim were sealed twelve thousand. Of the tribe of Manasses were sealed twelve thousand. Of the tribe of Simeon were sealed twelve thousand. Of the tribe of Levi were sealed twelve thousand. Of the tribe of Issachar were sealed twelve thousand. Of the tribe of Zabulon were sealed twelve thousand. Of the tribe of Joseph were sealed twelve thousand. Of the tribe of Benjamin were sealed twelve thousand."* — Rev 7:1-8

"And upon **Elam** *will I bring the four winds from the four quarters of heaven, and will scatter them toward all those winds; and there shall be no nation whither the outcasts of* **Elam** *shall not come."* — Jeremiah 49:36.

Elam is modern-day Iran.

144,000 Jews are sealed in their foreheads by the Lord for service during the first 3 ½ years of the 7-year tribulation period. They are sealed prior to the angels releasing any destructive forces on the earth. They preach the Gospel of the Kingdom during the first half of the tribulation as the Lord spoke in Matthew 24.

*"And this **gospel of the kingdom shall be preached in all the world** for a witness unto all nations; and **then shall the end come.**" - Matthew 24:14 KJV*

*"After this I beheld, and, lo, **a great multitude**, which no man could number, of all nations, and kindreds, and people, and tongues, stood before the throne, and before the Lamb, **clothed with white robes, and palms in their hands; And cried with a loud voice, saying, Salvation to our God which sitteth upon the throne, and unto the Lamb.** And all the angels stood round about the throne, and about the elders and the four beasts, and fell before the throne on their faces, and worshipped God, Saying, Amen: Blessing, and glory, and wisdom, and thanksgiving, and honour, and power, and might, be unto our God for ever and ever. Amen. And one of the elders answered, saying unto me, **What are these which are arrayed in white robes?** and whence came they? And I said unto him, Sir, thou knowest. And he said to me, **These are they which came out of great tribulation, and have washed their robes, and made them white in the blood of the Lamb**. Therefore are they before the throne of God, **and serve him day and night in his temple:** and he that sitteth on the throne shall dwell among them. They shall hunger no more, neither thirst any more; neither shall the sun light on them, nor any heat. For the Lamb which is in the midst of the throne shall feed them, and shall lead them unto living fountains of waters: and God shall wipe away all tears from their eyes." — Rev 7:9-17*

A great multitude from every nation stand before the Lord, clothed in white, worshiping the Lord; who are these? They are tribulation saints; those believers that died during the tribulation and will now serve the Lord in the temple. These are not part of the Church, the body of Christ, as we are already in heaven having been raptured before the Tribulation began.

Chaptër Twënty Twä
Thë Sëvën Trumpëts

The First Trumpet Judgment:

"And when he had opened the **seventh seal,** *there was silence in heaven about the space of half an hour. And I saw the seven angels which stood before God; and to them were given* **seven trumpets.** *And another angel came and stood at the altar, having a golden censer; and there was given unto him much incense, that he should offer it with the prayers of all saints upon the golden altar which was before the throne. And the smoke of the incense, which came with the prayers of the saints, ascended up before God out of the angel's hand. And* **the angel took the censer, and filled it with fire of the altar, and cast it into the earth: and there were voices, and thunderings, and lightnings, and an earthquake.** *And the seven angels which had the seven trumpets prepared themselves to sound.* **The first angel sounded, and there followed hail and fire mingled with blood, and they were cast upon the earth: and the third part of trees was burnt up, and all green grass was burnt up."* — *Rev 8:1-7*

"Thou shalt be visited of the LORD of hosts **with thunder,** *and* **with earthquake,** *and* **great noise,** *with* **storm and tempest,** *and the* **flame of devouring fire."** — *Isaiah 29:6 (This is a visitation upon Israel when she is overrun by her enemies in the last days)*

"And I will shew wonders in the heavens and in the earth, **blood,** *and fire, and* **pillars of smoke."** — *Joel 2:30*

183

*"Hast thou entered into the treasures of the snow? or hast thou seen the **treasures of the hail**, Which I have reserved against the **time of trouble, against the day of battle and war**?"* — *Job 38:22-23*

*"He gave them **hail** for rain, and **flaming fire** in their land."* — *Psalm 105:32 (Moses in Egypt)*

*"O LORD, to thee will I cry: for the **fire hath devoured the pastures** of the wilderness, and the **flame hath burned all the trees of the field.**"* — *Joel 1:19*

*"Therefore thus saith the Lord GOD; Behold, **mine anger and my fury shall be poured out upon this place**, upon man, and upon beast, and **upon the trees of the field**, and upon **the fruit of the ground; and it shall burn**, and shall not be quenched."* — *Jeremiah 7:20*

This scenario could be a nuclear exchange doing limited damage. Thunder, lightning, earthquakes, hailstorms, and fire mixed with blood is cast to the earth. One third of vegetation in the region of Israel is destroyed, but only temporarily.

The Second Trumpet Judgment:

*"And the **second angel sounded**, and as it were a **great mountain burning with fire was cast into the sea: and the third part of the sea became blood**; And the third part of the creatures which were in the sea, and had life, died; and the **third part of the ships were destroyed.**"* — *Rev 8:8-9*

This "great mountain" could be a large volcano. There are many active volcanoes in the Middle East area. A large volcanic eruption could easily pollute areas of the Mediterranean or Red Sea and kill a significant percentage of fish and other creatures of the deep. This type of catastrophe could also damage and disrupt shipping.

*"The mountains quake at him, and the **hills melt**, and the **earth is burned** at his presence, yea, the world, and all that dwell therein."*— *Nahum 1:5*

*"Oh that thou wouldest rend the heavens, that thou wouldest come down, that the **mountains might flow down** at thy presence,"* — *Isaiah 64:1*

*"The **hills melted** like wax at the presence of the LORD, at the presence of the Lord of the whole earth."* — *Psalm 97:5*

The Third Trumpet Judgment:

*"And the **third angel sounded**, and there **fell a great star from heaven**, burning as it were a lamp, and **it fell upon the third part of the rivers, and upon the fountains of waters**; And the name of the star is called Wormwood: and the third part of the waters became wormwood; and **many men died** of the waters, because they were made **bitter**."* — *Rev 8:10-11*

This great star from heaven could be an asteroid or comet. If an asteroid or comet collided with the earth it would produce atmospheric heat shock causing oxygen and nitrogen to combine into nitric acid rain. This rain falling over the headwaters of the Tigris and Euphrates rivers would potentially poison the water supply for millions of people in Turkey, Syria, and Iraq.

185

"How art thou fallen from heaven, O Lucifer, son of the morning! how art thou cut down to the ground, which didst weaken the nations!" — Isaiah 14:12

This could also have a spiritual interpretation. The fallen star could be Satan, who poisons (wormwood) a third of the waters (people in the Middle East), they believe his lie and die spiritually and physically from drinking his poison.

The Fourth Trumpet Judgment:

*"And the **fourth angel sounded**, and the **third part of the sun was smitten**, and the **third part of the moon, and the third part of the stars; so as the third part of them was darkened**, and the day shone not for a third part of it, and the night likewise. And I beheld, and heard an angel flying through the midst of heaven, saying with a loud voice, **Woe, woe, woe, to the inhabiters of the earth by reason of the other voices of the trumpet of the three angels, which are yet to sound!**"* — Rev 8:12-13

*"Behold, the day of the LORD cometh, cruel both with wrath and fierce anger, to lay the land desolate: and he shall destroy the sinners thereof out of it. For the **stars of heaven** and the **constellations** thereof **shall not give their light**: the **sun shall be darkened** in his going forth, and the **moon shall not cause her light to shine**."* — Isaiah 13:9-10

*"Then the **moon shall be confounded, and the sun ashamed**, when the LORD of hosts shall reign in mount Zion, and in Jerusalem, and before his ancients gloriously."* — Isaiah 24:23

*"And when I shall put thee out, I will cover the heaven, and **make the stars thereof dark; I will cover the sun with a cloud, and the moon shall not give her light**." — Ezekiel 32:7(spoken against Egypt)*

*"The earth shall quake before them; the heavens shall tremble: **the sun and the moon shall be dark, and the stars shall withdraw their shining**:" — Joel 2:10*

*"The **sun shall be turned into darkness, and the moon into blood, before the great and the terrible day of the LORD come**." — Joel 2:31*

*"Immediately after the tribulation of those days shall **the sun be darkened, and the moon shall not give her light, and the stars shall fall from heaven**, and the powers of the heavens shall be shaken:" — Mat 24:29*

The sun, moon and stars are darkened by one third probably from the tremendous atmospheric disturbances and pollution from the volcanic eruption and the impact from the meteor/comet.

Woe, woe, woe – it only gets worse.

The Fifth Trumpet Judgment:

*"And the **fifth angel sounded**, and I saw a **star fall from heaven unto the earth**: and to him was given the **key of the bottomless pit**. And he opened the bottomless pit; and there arose a smoke out of the pit, as the smoke of a great furnace; and the sun and the air were darkened by reason of the smoke of the pit. And **there came out of the smoke locusts upon the earth**: and unto them was given power, as the **scorpions** of the earth have power. And it was commanded them that*

*they should **not hurt the grass of the earth, neither any green thing**, neither any tree; but **only those men which have not the seal of God in their foreheads**. And to them it was given that they should not kill them, but that **they should be tormented five months**: and their torment was as the torment of a scorpion, when he striketh a man. And in those days **shall men seek death**, and shall not find it; and shall desire to die, and death shall flee from them. And the **shapes of the locusts were like unto horses prepared unto battle**; and on their heads were as it were **crowns like gold**, and their faces were as the **faces of men**. And they had hair as the **hair of women**, and their teeth were **as the teeth of lions**. And they had breastplates, as it were **breastplates of iron**; and the sound of their wings was as the sound of chariots of many horses running to battle. And they had **tails like unto scorpions**, and there were stings in their tails: and their power was to **hurt men five months**. And **they had a king over them, which is the angel of the bottomless pit, whose name in the Hebrew tongue is Abaddon, but in the Greek tongue hath his name Apollyon**. One woe is past; and, behold, there come two woes more hereafter."* — Rev 9:1-12*

This trumpet woe is profoundly serious. A star (angel) comes from heaven with the key to the bottomless pit (subterranean chamber of hell) and opens the pit. The entrance to the bottomless pit is thought to be in the Euphrates River valley because of the next woe (v. 13-21). Physically this could be a fissure opening and releasing smoke and gasses from within the earth. Spiritually, hosts of horrendously evil spirits are released on mankind, all except the 144,000 sealed with the seal of God.

These creatures are as locusts, but they do not hurt anything green, exactly the opposite of real locusts. They have power over the earth to hurt men for five months. Their inflicted pain will be so great that men will seek death, but death will elude them. This trumpet is a direct judgment from God.

These creatures have the following characteristics:
- do not eat grass or anything green.
- have power over men.
- like battle horses.
- Crowned.
- face of a man.
- hair like a woman.
- teeth of a lion.
- breastplates of iron.
- scorpion like tails.

These creatures have a king. Psalm 30:27 states that locusts have no king, so these are demonic. These stinging locust-like demons are led by Apollyon, whose name means "destroyer", to torment mankind for five months. Allah, the moon god of Islam, has a title of Al-Mumeet meaning "the destroyer."

*"Rejoice not thou, whole Palestina, because the rod of him that smote thee is broken: **for out of the serpent's root shall come forth a cockatrice and his fruit shall be a fiery flying serpent**." — Isaiah 14:29*

These serpents are demonic beings sent from hell by God to torture unbelieving mankind for 5 months.

The Sixth Trumpet Judgment:

*"And the **sixth angel sounded**, and I heard a voice from the four horns of the golden altar which is before God, Saying to the sixth angel which had the trumpet, **Loose the four angels which are bound in the great river Euphrates**. And the four angels were loosed, which were prepared for an **hour, and a day, and a month, and a year, for to slay the third part of men**. **And the number of the army of the horsemen were two hundred thousand thousand**: and I heard the*

*number of them. And thus I saw the horses in the vision, and them that sat on them, having **breastplates of fire, and of jacinth, and brimstone: and the heads of the horses were as the heads of lions; and out of their mouths issued fire and smoke and brimstone**. By these three was the third part of men killed, by the fire, and by the smoke, and by the brimstone, which issued out of their mouths. For **their power is in their mouth, and in their tails:** for their tails were like unto serpents, and had heads, and with them they do hurt. And the rest of the men which were not killed by these plagues yet repented not of the works of their hands, that they should not worship devils, and idols of gold, and silver, and brass, and stone, and of wood: which neither can see, nor hear, nor walk: Neither repented they of their murders, nor of their sorceries, nor of their fornication, nor of their thefts." — Rev 9:13-21*

A great army is gathered in the area of the Euphrates River to kill a third of mankind in the Middle East. This great river flows through Iraq (Babylon), Syria (Assyria) and Turkey (Asia Minor).

John is describing in first century lingo another great demonic army arising from the Euphrates River to kill a third of men. However, Israel is not mentioned in the text so this probably is not an invasion of Israel. Even though a third of men in this area are killed, none repent of the evil works. This is another plague from God to motivate man to repent.

"Upon the wicked he shall rain snares, fire and brimstone, and an horrible tempest: this shall be the portion of their cup." — Psalm 11:6

"And I will plead against him with pestilence and with blood; and I will rain upon him, and upon his bands, and upon the many people that are with him, an overflowing rain, and great hailstones, fire, and brimstone." — Ezekiel 38:22

*"Come up, ye horses; and rage, ye chariots; and let the mighty men come forth; the **Ethiopians** and the **Libyans**, that handle the shield; and the **Lydians,** that handle and bend the bow. For this is **the day of the Lord GOD of hosts**, a day of vengeance, that he may avenge him of his adversaries: and the sword shall devour, and it shall be satiate and made drunk with their blood: for **the Lord GOD of hosts hath a sacrifice in the north country by the river Euphrates.**"* — Jeremiah 46:9-10*

The seals and trumpets portray an ever-increasing judgment being poured out upon the earth for the purpose of driving man to repentance through judgment.

*"And I saw **another mighty angel come down from heaven**, clothed with a cloud: and a rainbow was upon his head, and his face was as it were the sun, and his feet as pillars of fire: And he had in his hand a little book open: and he set his right foot upon the sea, and his left foot on the earth, And cried with a loud voice, as when a lion roareth: and when he had cried, seven thunders uttered their voices. And when the seven thunders had uttered their voices, I was about to write: and I heard a voice from heaven saying unto me, **Seal up those things which the seven thunders uttered, and write them not.** And the angel which I saw stand upon the sea and upon the earth lifted up his hand to heaven, And sware by him that liveth for ever and ever, who created heaven, and the things that therein are, and the earth, and the things that therein are, and the sea, and the things which are therein, that there should be time no longer: **But in the days of the voice of the seventh angel, when he shall begin to sound, the mystery of God should be finished, as he hath declared to his servants the prophets.** And the voice which I heard from heaven spake unto me again, and said, Go and take the little book which is open in the hand of the angel which standeth upon the sea and upon the earth. And I went*

191

unto the angel, and said unto him, Give me the little book. And he said unto me, Take it, and eat it up; and it shall make thy belly bitter, but it shall be in thy mouth sweet as honey. And I took the little book out of the angel's hand, and ate it up; and it was in my mouth sweet as honey: and as soon as I had eaten it, my belly was bitter. And he said unto me, Thou must prophesy again before many peoples, and nations, and tongues, and kings." — Rev 10:1-11

Some things will remain sealed until the time of their fulfillment. The seventh trumpet will include the seven vials and take us through the fulfillment of the day of the Lord prophecies. The mystery of God could refer to the unfolding of the entire plan of God for the ages.

*"Repent ye therefore, and be converted, that your sins may be blotted out, when the **times of refreshing shall come from the presence of the Lord**; And he shall send Jesus Christ, which before was preached unto you: Whom the heaven must receive until the **times of restitution of all things**, which God hath spoken by the mouth of all his holy prophets since the world began." — Acts 3:19-21*

*"Now to him that is of power to stablish you according to my gospel, and the preaching of Jesus Christ, **according to the revelation of the mystery, which was kept secret since the world began,** But now is made manifest, and by the scriptures of the prophets, according to the commandment of the everlasting God, made known to all nations for the obedience of faith:"*
— Rom 16:25-26

*"And he said unto them, These are the words which I spake unto you, while I was yet with you, that **all things must be fulfilled**, which were written in the law of Moses, and in the prophets, and in the psalms, concerning me." — Luke 24:44*

Times of the Gentiles:

"And there was given me a reed like unto a rod: and the angel stood, saying, **Rise, and measure the temple of God, and the altar, and them that worship therein.** **But the court which is without the temple leave out, and measure it not; for it is given unto the Gentiles***: and the holy city shall they tread under foot* **forty and two months.***" — Rev 11:1-2*

The Temple Mount Eastern Gate is currently sealed. If you look at any good image of the temple mount and eastern gate you will notice that the area of the mount directly behind the eastern gate is vacant. This area is the site of Solomon's and Herod's Temple not including the outer court. Notice that the text says that the outer court is given to the gentiles. The Muslim Dome of the Rock is sitting in the outer court. The Hebrew Temple will be rebuilt during the first 3 ½ years of the tribulation. I believe it will be adjacent to the Dome of the Rock.

Two Witnesses:

"And I will give power unto **my two witnesses,** *and they shall prophesy a* **thousand two hundred and threescore days,** *clothed in sackcloth.* *These are the* **two olive trees, and the two candlesticks standing before the God of the earth.** *And if any man will hurt them, fire proceedeth out of their mouth, and devoureth their enemies: and if any man will hurt them, he must in this manner be killed. These have power to* **shut heaven, that it rain not** *in the days of their prophecy: and have* **power over waters to turn them to blood,** *and to smite the earth with all plagues, as often as they will. And when they shall have finished their testimony,* **the beast that ascendeth out of the bottomless pit shall make war against them, and shall overcome them, and kill them.** *And their dead bodies shall lie in the street of the great city, which spiritually is called Sodom and Egypt, where also*

193

our Lord was crucified. And they of the people and kindreds and tongues and **nations shall see their dead bodies three days and an half***, and shall not suffer their dead bodies to be put in graves. And they that dwell upon the earth shall rejoice over them, and make merry, and shall send gifts one to another; because these two prophets tormented them that dwelt on the earth.* **And after three days and an half the Spirit of life from God entered into them, and they stood upon their feet***; and great fear fell upon them which saw them. And they heard a great voice from heaven saying unto them,* **Come up hither. And they ascended up to heaven in a cloud; and their enemies beheld them.**" — *Rev 11:3-12*

"Then answered I, and said unto him, **What are these two olive trees upon the right side of the candlestick and upon the left side thereof?** *And I answered again, and said unto him,* **What be these two olive branches which through the two golden pipes empty the golden oil out of themselves?** *And he answered me and said, Knowest thou not what these be? And I said, No, my lord. Then said he,* **These are the two anointed ones, that stand by the Lord of the whole earth.**" — *Zechariah 4:11-14*

Two olive trees are Moses and Elijah. They torment people with the gospel of the kingdom, the truth. It is amazing that today truth is the new hate speech; everything is upside down. The two witnesses are protected by the power of God for 3 ½ years, probably the first half of the tribulation. They can stop the rain, turn water to blood and many other plagues. The beast from the bottomless pit (Satan empowered Antichrist) will finally kill them. Their dead bodies will lie in the street in Jerusalem for 3 ½ days. People will cheer and send gifts celebrating their death. Then they will rise to their feet and all will be in fear. The Lord calls them to heaven, and they ascend in view of their enemies. Wow, can you imagine the coverage of this by the talking heads on the alphabet television news networks?

*"And the same hour was there a great earthquake, and the **tenth part of the city fell,** and in the earthquake were slain of men seven thousand: and the **remnant were affrighted, and gave glory to the God of heaven.** The second woe is past; and, behold, the third woe cometh quickly." — Rev 11:13-14*

After the two witnesses ascend to heaven there is a great earthquake and one tenth of Jerusalem is destroyed. The remnant of Israel still alive is frightened but still glorifies the Lord of heaven.

The Seventh Trumpet Judgment:

*"And the **seventh angel sounded;** and there were great voices in heaven, saying, **The kingdoms of this world are become the kingdoms of our Lord, and of his Christ; and he shall reign for ever and ever.** And the four and twenty elders, which sat before God on their seats, fell upon their faces, and worshipped God, Saying, We give thee thanks, O Lord God Almighty, which art, and wast, and art to come; because thou hast taken to thee thy great power, and hast reigned. And **the nations were angry, and thy wrath is come,** and the time of the dead, that they should be judged, and that thou shouldest give reward unto thy servants the prophets, and to the saints, and them that fear thy name, small and great; and **shouldest destroy them which destroy the earth.** And the temple of God was opened in heaven, and there was seen in his temple the ark of his testament: and there were **lightnings,** and voices, and **thunderings,** and an **earthquake,** and **great hail."** — Rev 11:15-19*

The seventh trumpet proclaims the kingdoms of the world have become the kingdoms of the Father and the Lord Jesus Christ who will reign forever. But the evil nations are angry and do not want Jesus to rule and reign. However, the Lord Jesus will destroy those nations that are destroying the earth. We have already studied many verses in the Old Testament pertaining to the destruction of nations by the Lord at His return. The seventh trumpet contains the seven bowls just as the seventh seal contained the seven trumpets.

Trumpet judgment summary:

1st Trumpet	Hail, fire mixed with blood	Third part of trees burnt up and all grass
2nd Trumpet	Great mountain burning with fire	Third part of the sea became blood
3rd Trumpet	Great star falls from heaven	Third part of the rivers became blood
4th Trumpet	Third part of the sun, moon and stars smitten	Day and night darkened
5th Trumpet	Angel opens the bottom pit	Demon locusts released up the earth
6th Trumpet	Euphrates River dries up	Kings of the east come to battle at Armageddon
7th Trumpet	Great voices and worship in heaven	Second Coming of the Lord Jesus

Chäptër Twënty Thrëë

Prämïnënt Përsäns

*"And there appeared a **great wonder in heaven; a woman clothed with the sun, and the moon under her feet, and upon her head a crown of twelve stars: And she being with child** cried, travailing in birth, and pained to be delivered. And there appeared another wonder in heaven; and behold a **great red dragon**, having **seven heads and ten horns**, and seven crowns upon his heads. And his tail drew the third part of the stars of heaven, and did cast them to the earth: and the dragon stood before the woman which was ready to be delivered, for to **devour her child as soon as it was born**. And **she brought forth a man child**, who was **to rule all nations with a rod of iron:** and her child was **caught up** unto God, and to his throne. And the **woman fled into the wilderness,** where she hath a place prepared of God, that they should feed her there **a thousand two hundred and threescore days**."* — Rev 12:1-6

A Great Wonder appears in the heavens. The real stuff is in heaven; the things of God on earth are mere representations of the true reality in heaven. The woman clothed with the sun and the moon under her feet and the crown of twelve stars on her head is Israel. Israel gave birth to the Messiah. "For unto us (Israel) a child is born…" Isaiah 9:6. The twelve stars represent the twelve patriarchs/tribes. The moon under her feet could represent Israel's complete victory over Islam.

The red dragon is Satan and the fallen angels he brought with him from heaven. We will see the red dragon later.

The seven heads are explained later in Revelation chapter seventeen, but for now understand that these seven heads are seven earthly kingdoms. The ten horns correspond to the 10 toes of the image in Daniel 2, the 10 horns of the fourth beast in Daniel 7 and the 10 horned beast of Revelation 13. These represent the 10 nation Middle Eastern confederacy the Antichrist will rule during his 3 ½ year reign of terror in the Great Tribulation (last half of the 7-year tribulation).

The woman's child is Jesus who, at his second coming, will rule the nations with a rod of iron. The child is "caught up" to God; this is the same Greek word used in 1st Thessalonians chapter 4 for the saints being "caught up" in the Rapture.

During the last 3 ½ years of the tribulation Israel will flee into the wilderness to a place prepared for her by God to endure the last 3 ½ years plus 30 days. Jesus spoke of this in Matthew 24 when he said:

*"When ye therefore shall see the **abomination of desolation, spoken of by Daniel the prophet,** stand in the holy place, (whoso readeth, let him understand:) **Then let them which be in Judaea flee into the mountains:"** — Mat 24:15-16*

This event is in the middle of the 7-year tribulation. For the last half of the Tribulation the remnant of Israel will be protected from the Antichrist by God.

*"And there was **war in heaven: Michael and his angels fought against the dragon;** and the dragon fought and his angels, And prevailed not; neither was their place found any more in heaven. And **the great dragon was cast out, that old serpent, called the Devil, and Satan, which deceiveth the whole world: he was cast out into the earth,** and his angels were cast out with him. And I heard a loud voice saying in heaven, Now is come salvation, and strength, and the kingdom of our God, and the power of his Christ: for the **accuser of our brethren is cast down, which accused them before our God day and night. And they overcame him by the blood***

of the Lamb, and by the word of their testimony; and they loved not their lives unto the death. Therefore rejoice, ye heavens, and ye that dwell in them. **Woe to the inhabiters of the earth** and of the sea! for the **devil is come down unto you,** having **great wrath,** because he knoweth that he hath but a **short time.**" — *Rev 12:7-12*

During the entire time of man on the earth, Satan has had access to the throne of God to accuse the brethren. Finally, at the middle of the seven-year tribulation he is cast out of heaven. There is a war in heaven and Michael prevails casting Satan and his angels to the earth. This is the time when Satan personally empowers the Antichrist. We will see this in the Revelation chapter 13.

*"**In that day the LORD** with his sore and great and strong sword shall **punish leviathan the piercing serpent,** even leviathan that **crooked serpent**; and he shall **slay the dragon** that is in the sea."* — *Isaiah 27:1*

*"And when the dragon saw that he was cast unto the earth, **he persecuted the woman which brought forth the man child.** And to the woman were given two wings of a great eagle, that she might fly into the wilderness, into her place, **where she is nourished for a time, and times, and half a time, from the face of the serpent.** And the serpent cast out of his mouth water as a flood after the woman, that he might cause her to be carried away of the flood. And the earth helped the woman, and the earth opened her mouth, and swallowed up the flood which the dragon cast out of his mouth. And the dragon was wroth with the woman, **and went to make war with the remnant of her seed,** which keep the commandments of God, and have the testimony of Jesus Christ."* — *Rev 12:13-17*

The dragon, Satan persecutes the woman, Israel. Israel escapes from the dragon into the wilderness to a place prepared for her by God and is protected there for 3 ½ years. The dragon's wrath is great towards Israel, but the remnant is protected.

Zechariah tells us in chapter 13:8-9 that in the final invasion of Israel two thirds will perish in the battle but a third will survive.

*"And it shall come to pass, that in all the land, saith the LORD, **two parts therein shall be cut off and die; but the third shall be left therein.** And I will bring the **third part through the fire,** and will refine them as silver is refined, and will try them as gold is tried: they shall call on my name, and I will hear them: I will say, It is my people: and they shall say, The LORD is my God."*

Chapter 13 of Revelation reveals two beasts. The Antichrist and the False Prophet. Two members of the end times Satanic trinity.

*"And I stood upon the **sand of the sea,** and saw a **beast rise up out of the sea,** having **seven heads and ten horns,** and upon his horns ten crowns, and upon his heads the name of blasphemy. And the **beast which I saw was like unto a leopard,** and his feet were as **the feet of a bear,** and his mouth as the **mouth of a lion: and the dragon gave him his power, and his seat, and great authority.** And I saw **one of his heads as it were wounded to death; and his deadly wound was healed:** and all the world wondered after the beast. And they worshipped the dragon which gave power unto the beast: and they worshipped the beast, saying, Who is like unto the beast? who is able to make war with him? And there was given unto him a **mouth speaking great things and blasphemies;** and power was given unto him to **continue forty and two months.** And he opened his mouth in blasphemy against God, to blaspheme his name, and his tabernacle,*

*and them that dwell in heaven. And it was given unto him to **make war with the saints, and to overcome them**: and power was given him over all kindreds, and tongues, and nations. And **all that dwell upon the earth shall worship him**, whose names are not written in the book of life of the Lamb slain from the foundation of the world. If any man have an ear, let him hear. He that leadeth into captivity shall go into captivity: he that killeth with the sword must be killed with the sword. Here is the patience and the faith of the saints." — Rev 13:1-10*

The Beast that arises from the sea is described for us in Daniel chapter 7.

- o Like a Leopard – Kingdom of Greece (Asia Minor) Dan 7:6
- o Feet of a Bear – Kingdom of Persia (Iran) Dan 7:5
- o Mouth of a Lion – Kingdom of Babylon (Iraq) Dan 7:4

This Beast of Revelation 13:1-10 is the 4th beast of Daniel chapter 7, and the feet of iron and clay of the image in Daniel chapter 2. It is a composite of the ancient geographical areas of Asia Minor, Babylon, and Persia.

The Sea is not the Mediterranean Sea or any other body of water; it is the sea of nations in the Middle East. The beast kingdom has 7 heads and 10 horns. The 4th beast of Daniel chapter 7 also has 10 horns. The ten horns are 10 kings that will arise and give their power to the Antichrist.

Notice that one of the 7 heads is wounded unto death and is later healed. This could be both a wounded and somehow resurrected Antichrist and a wounded and revived kingdom. The seven heads are the seven kingdoms that have risen to control the Middle East: Egypt, Assyria, Babylon, Media-Persia, Greece, Islamic/Ottoman Empire and the revived Islamic/Ottoman empire. This will be discussed in greater length in Revelation chapter 17 and 18. But for now let me just say that the 7th empire is the wounded Islamic (Ottoman) empire. This happened in

1924 when the Ottoman Caliphate was dissolved after WW1. This wounded Islamic Caliphate will come back to life in the near future as a 10-nation confederacy. There is a desire by many in the Islamic world to reinstate the Caliphate with Turkey at the center. The Muslim Brotherhood was formed in 1928 for this exact purpose, to re-establish the Islamic Caliphate.

Psalm 83 speaks of a Confederacy of nations that come against Israel:

*"For, lo, thine enemies make a tumult: and they that hate thee have lifted up the head. They have **taken crafty counsel against thy people,** and consulted against thy hidden ones. They have said, **Come, and let us cut them off from being a nation; that the name of Israel may be no more in remembrance.** For they have consulted together with one consent: **they are confederate against thee:** The tabernacles of Edom, and the Ishmaelites; of Moab, and the Hagarenes; Gebal, and Ammon, and Amalek; the Philistines with the inhabitants of Tyre; Assur also is joined with them: they have holpen the children of Lot. Selah."*

The Gog alliance of Ezekiel 38, Meshech, Tubal (Turkey), Persia, Ethiopia (Sudan), Libya, and more all come against Israel in the last days. Add to these the Islamic Confederacy mentioned in Psalm 83, Jordan, Arabia, Lebanon, Gaza, Syria, Turkey, Iran, Sudan, Libya, and Iraq. These 10 nations are aligned against Israel.

Getting back to the text, the mouth speaking great blasphemies given to the beast kingdom is the Antichrist. He is given power to reign over this beast kingdom for 3 ½ years (42 months). During that time, Antichrist will persecute believers and overcome them. He will be worshiped by the Muslims, all whose names are not written in the Lamb's Book of Life.

Daniel states in 7:25, 21

*"And **he shall speak great words against the most High**, and **shall wear out the saints of the most High**, and think to **change times and laws**: and they shall be given into his hand until a **time and times and the dividing of time**."*

*"I beheld, and **the same horn made war with the saints, and prevailed against them**;"*

Note that Islam seeks to change times and laws by imposing Sharia law on those it subjugates. Here again we see the 3 ½ year duration of the Antichrists evil reign (time, times and half a time).

Summary of the first beast:
- A Beast Kingdom that arises in the Middle East.
- Composite of the ancient geographical areas of Assyria, Babylon, and Persia.
- Revived 10 nation Caliphate lead by the Antichrist.
- Reigns for 3 ½ years (last half of the 7-year tribulation.
- Blasphemes the Lord and overcomes the saints.

*"And I beheld **another beast coming up out of the earth; and he had two horns like a lamb, and he spake as a dragon**. And he exerciseth all the power of the first beast before him, and causeth the earth and them which dwell therein to **worship the first beast, whose deadly wound was healed**. And he doeth **great wonders**, so that **he maketh fire come down from heaven** on the earth in the sight of men, And **deceiveth them that dwell on the earth** by the means of those miracles which he had power to do in the sight of the beast; saying to them that dwell on the earth, that they should make an **image to the beast**, which had the wound by a sword, and did live. And he had power **to give life unto the image of the beast**, that the image of the beast*

203

*should both speak, and cause that as many as would not worship the image of the beast should be **killed**. And he causeth all, both small and great, rich and poor, free and bond, to receive a **mark in their right hand, or in their foreheads**: And that no man might buy or sell, save he that **had the mark**, or **the name of the beast, or the number of his name**. Here is wisdom. Let him that hath understanding count the number of the beast: for it is the number of a man; and his number is Six hundred threescore and six."* — Rev 13:11-18

This beast is obviously a man. He has two horns like a lamb implying that he is a lamb-like messiah, but he speaks like a dragon, like Satan. This is the False Prophet.

All that dwell in the land must swear allegiance to the Antichrist kingdom. The Antichrist and False Prophet will perform great lying wonders to deceive those that dwell in the land. An image of the kingdom is created, and the False Prophet is able to give life to the image. Since we are talking about the satanically empowered Antichrist and False Prophet, this is probably not a mere technological trick, but a real deceiving miracle.

To show their allegiance, all must wear the badge of servitude (mark) on their forehead or right arm. No one will be able to buy or sell without the badge of servitude on their arm or forehead OR profess the name of the Antichrist (Caliph) OR professing the name of the multitude (Caliphate). Please refer to the Mark of the Beast section.

Chapter Twenty Four
The Harvest of the Wicked

"And I looked, and, lo, **a Lamb stood on the mount Sion, and with him an hundred forty and four thousand, having his Father's name written in their foreheads.** *And I heard a voice from heaven, as the voice of many waters, and as the voice of a great thunder: and I heard the voice of harpers harping with their harps: And they sung as it were a* **new song** *before the throne, and before the four beasts, and the elders: and no man could learn that song but the hundred and forty and four thousand, which were redeemed from the earth. These are they which were not defiled with women; for they are virgins. These are they which follow the Lamb whithersoever he goeth. These were* **redeemed from among men, being the firstfruits unto God and to the Lamb.** *And in their mouth was found no guile: for they are without fault* **before the throne of God.***"*
— *Rev 14:1-5*

This is a picture of the 144,000 in heaven before the throne of God for their work on earth is finished. They are the firstfruits of the tribulation saints.

"And I saw another **angel fly in the midst of heaven, having the everlasting gospel to preach unto them that dwell on the earth,** *and to every nation, and kindred, and tongue, and people, Saying with a loud voice,* **Fear God, and give glory to him; for the hour of his judgment is come: and worship him that made heaven, and earth, and the sea, and the fountains of waters.** *And there followed another angel, saying,* **Babylon is fallen, is fallen, that great city,**

because she made all nations drink of the wine of the wrath of her fornication. And the third angel followed them, saying with a loud voice, **If any man worship the beast and his image, and receive his mark in his forehead, or in his hand, The same shall drink of the wine of the wrath of God,** *which is poured out without mixture into the cup of his indignation; and he shall be tormented with fire and brimstone in the presence of the holy angels, and in the presence of the Lamb:* **And the smoke of their torment ascendeth up for ever and ever:** *and they have no rest day nor night, who worship the beast and his image, and whosoever receiveth the mark of his name."— Rev 14:6-11*

Could the angel flying in the midst of heaven be a satellite? Hot Bird 8 currently hovers over the Middle East preaching the gospel 24/7.

"Babylon is fallen, is fallen." Is a direct quote from Isaiah 21:9. Chapter 21 of Isaiah begins with the "burden of the desert of the sea" then "the burden of Dumah" and concludes with the "burden of Arabia." These all speak of the Arabian Peninsula. But how is Babylon associated with Arabia?

Babylon is a symbolic code word. Original Babylon on the Euphrates River was the seat of all pagan religions and idolatry going back to the tower of Babel. However, over the centuries the seat of pagan religion in the Middle East shifted. During these last days the pagan religion of the Middle East is Islam.

Mecca is the holy city of Islam so now the "Babylon" of the Middle East is Mecca. Certainly not coincidental, Mecca is on the Arabian Peninsula in the Arabian desert. What is "the wine" she is making us drink? Oil. What is she exporting with all that money? Islam and terrorism.

Here also Babylon (Mecca) is associated with the mark (badge of servitude) of the beast. Anyone wearing it will drink the wine of the wrath of God.

"The smoke of their torment shall ascend up for ever and ever" is a quote from Isaiah:

*"For it is the **day of the LORD'S vengeance,** and the year of recompences for the controversy of Zion. And the streams thereof shall be **turned into pitch,** and the dust thereof into brimstone, and **the land thereof shall become burning pitch.** It shall not be quenched night nor day; **the smoke thereof shall go up forever:** from generation to generation it shall lie waste; none shall pass through it for ever and ever."* — Isaiah 34:8-10

*"The earth is moved at the **noise of their fall,** at the cry the noise thereof was **heard in the Red sea."** — Jeremiah 49:21 (Concerning Edom – Jordan and Arabia)*

The destruction of Mecca will be easily seen from the Red Sea, not so with ancient Babylon. Since Arabia is the world's leading oil producer, it is easy to see how the land becomes burning pitch and the smoke of her burning will go up forever.

*"Here is the patience of the saints: here are they that keep the commandments of God, and the faith of Jesus. And I heard a voice from heaven saying unto me, Write, **Blessed are the dead which die in the Lord from henceforth:** Yea, saith the Spirit, that they may rest from their labours; and their works do follow them. And I looked, and behold a white cloud, and upon the cloud one sat like unto the Son of man, having on his head a golden crown, and in his hand a sharp sickle. **And another angel came out of the temple, crying with a loud voice to him that sat on the cloud, Thrust in thy sickle, and reap: for the time is come for thee to reap; for the harvest of the earth is ripe.** And he that sat on the cloud thrust in his sickle on the earth; and the earth was reaped. And another angel came out of the temple which is in heaven, he also having a sharp sickle. And another*

angel came out from the altar, which had power over fire; and cried with a loud cry to him that had the sharp sickle, saying, Thrust in thy sharp sickle, and gather the clusters of the vine of the earth; for her grapes are fully ripe. And the angel thrust in his sickle into the earth, and gathered the vine of the earth, and **cast it into the great winepress of the wrath of God.** *And the winepress was trodden without the city, and blood came out of the winepress, even unto the horse bridles, by the space of a thousand and six hundred furlongs."* — *Rev 14:12-20*

This is the harvest of the wicked from the earth. It is found in Joel chapter 3.

"Proclaim ye this among **the Gentiles***; Prepare war, wake up the mighty men, let all the men of war draw near; let them come up:* **Beat your plowshares into swords, and your pruninghooks into spears:** *let the weak say, I am strong. Assemble yourselves, and come, all ye heathen, and gather yourselves together round about: thither cause thy mighty ones to come down, O LORD. Let the heathen be wakened, and come up to the valley of Jehoshaphat: for there will I sit to judge all the heathen round about.* **Put ye in the sickle, for the harvest is ripe:** *come, get you down; for* **the press is full, the fats overflow; for their wickedness is great.** *Multitudes, multitudes in the valley of decision: for the day of the LORD is near in the valley of decision."* — *Joel 3:9-14*

"Who is this that cometh from Edom, with dyed garments from Bozrah? *this that is glorious in his apparel, travelling in the greatness of his strength? I that speak in righteousness, mighty to save.* **Wherefore art thou red in thine apparel, and thy garments like him that treadeth in the winefat?** **I have trodden the winepress alone***; and of the people there was none with me: for I will tread them in*

*mine **anger**, and trample them in my **fury**; and **their blood shall be**
sprinkled upon my garments, and I will stain all my raiment. For
the **day of vengeance is in mine heart,** and the year of my redeemed is
come. And I looked, and there was none to help; and I wondered that
there was none to uphold: therefore mine own arm brought salvation
unto me; and my fury, it upheld me. And **I will tread down the**
people in mine anger, and make them drunk in my fury, and I will
bring down their strength to the earth."* – Isaiah 63:1-6

The wrath of God is being unleashed on the earth. If
your sins are not washed by the blood of Jesus, then they will be
judged by an Almighty God. In Isaiah chapter 63 the Lord is
pictured with garments stained with the blood of His enemies
upon returning from Edom (Bozrah), modern day Jordan. The
Lord Jesus is treading the winepress of the wrath of God. Jesus'
first coming was as the Son of Joseph, a suffering servant of God
the Father. At His second coming the "day of vengeance" is in
His heart and unleashes great anger upon the enemies of God
and Israel.

Chapter Twenty Five
The Seven Vials

"And I saw another sign in heaven, great and marvelous, **seven angels having the seven last plagues; for in them is filled up the wrath of God.** *And I saw as it were a sea of glass mingled with fire: and them that had gotten the* **victory over the beast, and over his image, and over his mark, and over the number of his name,** *stand on the sea of glass, having the harps of God. And they sing the* **song of Moses** *the servant of God, and the song of the Lamb, saying, Great and marvelous are thy works, Lord God Almighty; just and true are thy ways, thou King of saints. Who shall not fear thee, O Lord, and glorify thy name? for thou only art holy: for all nations shall come and worship before thee; for thy judgments are made manifest." — Rev 15:1-4*

These last seven plagues are seven vials of judgment from the winepress of God's wrath poured out in the earth. The people that have victory over the beast, his image, his mark, and his number (multitude) sing the song of Moses. They sing the song of Moses because the 70th week of Daniel (7-year tribulation) is fulfilled under the Mosaic covenant as shown in the chapter on the Rapture of the Church. The singers are not Christians, but saved, martyred Jews.

"And after that I looked, and, behold, the temple of the tabernacle of the testimony in heaven was opened: And **the seven angels came out of the temple, having the seven plagues,** *clothed in pure and white linen, and having their breasts girded with golden girdles. And one of the four beasts gave unto the seven angels* **seven golden vials full of**

211

the wrath of God, who liveth for ever and ever. And the temple was filled with smoke from the glory of God, and from his power; and no man was able to enter into the temple, till the seven plagues of the seven angels were fulfilled." — Rev 15:5-8

The seven vials full of God's wrath are about to be poured out on the earth.

The First Vial Judgment: Sores

"And I heard a great voice out of the temple saying to the seven angels, Go your ways, and **pour out the vials of the wrath of God upon the earth.** *And the* **first** *went, and poured out his vial upon the earth; and there fell a* **noisome and grievous sore upon the men which had the mark of the beast, and upon them which worshipped his image.**" — Rev 16:1-2*

"*earth*" – Strong's G1093 "ge"; country, land, mainland enclosed within fixed boundaries, territory or region. The context is local to the Middle East and not global.

Sore boils were poured out among those that have the mark (badge of servitude) of the beast. This is similar to the 6th plague of Egypt.

The Second Vial Judgment: Sea of Blood

"And the **second angel** *poured out his vial upon the* **sea**; *and it* **became as the blood of a dead man: and every living soul died in the sea.**" — Rev 16:3*

The second angel pours his vial, the sea becomes blood, and everything therein dies. This is similar to the 1st plague of Egypt. Also, this could be an expansion of the second trumpet judgment where only one third of the sea becomes blood. Which sea? "sea" Strong's G2281 "thalassa"; used specifically of the Mediterranean Sea or the Red Sea. The context here is local to the Middle East, not global. If the context is global then life on earth as we know it would cease due to a lack of oxygen production since most of the oxygen we breathe comes from the sea.

The Third Vial Judgment: Rivers of Blood

"And the **third angel** *poured out his vial upon the* **rivers and fountains of waters**; *and they* **became blood**. *And I heard the angel of the waters say, Thou art righteous, O Lord, which art, and wast, and shalt be, because thou hast judged thus.* **For they have shed the blood of saints and prophets, and thou hast given them blood to drink; for they are worthy.** *And I heard another out of the altar say, Even so, Lord God Almighty, true and righteous are thy judgments."* — *Rev 16:4-7*

The sea and the rivers and fountains of water are local to the Middle East, not global. They are specific to the Muslim nations that surround Israel and are under the control of the beast.

The Fourth Vial Judgment: Fire

"And the **fourth angel** *poured out his vial upon the* **sun**; *and power was given unto him to* **scorch men with fire**. *And men were scorched with* **great heat**, *and blasphemed the name of God, which hath power over these plagues: and they repented not to give him glory."* — *Rev 16:8-9*

The proponents of global warming will love this verse saying "I told you so..." We know that an increase in the sun activity generates an increase in gamma rays that disturb the

213

electromagnetic forces in the earth. This activity warms the atmosphere and increases the intensity of the sun's heat on the earth. Even though men are scorched with heat they still won't repent.

The Fifth Vial Judgment: Darkness

*"And the **fifth angel** poured out his vial upon the **seat of the beast**; and **his kingdom was full of darkness**; and they gnawed their tongues for pain, And blasphemed the God of heaven because of their pains and their sores, and repented not of their deeds." — Rev 16:10-11*

*"Blow ye the trumpet in Zion, and sound an alarm in my holy mountain: let all the inhabitants of the land tremble: for **the day of the LORD cometh, for it is nigh at hand; A day of darkness and of gloominess, a day of clouds and of thick darkness**…" — Joel 2:1-2*

*"**The great day of the LORD is near**, it is near, and hasteth greatly, even the voice of the day of the LORD: the mighty man shall cry there bitterly. **That day is a day of wrath**, a day of trouble and distress, a day of wasteness and desolation, **a day of darkness and gloominess, a day of clouds and thick darkness**…" — Zephaniah 1:14-15*

This is absolutely a thick darkness of evil that oppresses the body and soul (heart and mind). The context being spiritual darkness so thick and overpowering you can sense it. Also, this darkness is a physical darkness due to the gross evil in the Middle East possibly similar to the darkness that accompanied the crucifixion of the Lord Jesus Christ.

*"Now from the sixth hour there was **darkness over all the land unto the ninth hour**. And about the ninth hour Jesus cried with a loud*

214

voice, saying, Eli, Eli, lama sabachthani? that is to say, My God, my God, why hast thou forsaken me?" — Matthew 27:45-46

The Sixth Vial Judgment: Devils

*"And the **sixth angel** poured out his vial upon the **great river Euphrates**; and the **water thereof was dried up**, that the way of the kings of the east might be prepared. And I saw **three unclean spirits like frogs come out of the mouth of the dragon**, and out of the **mouth of the beast**, and out of the **mouth of the False Prophet**. For they are the **spirits of devils**, working miracles, which go forth unto the kings of the earth and of the whole world, **to gather them to the battle of that great day of God Almighty**. Behold, I come as a thief. Blessed is he that watcheth, and keepeth his garments, lest he walk naked, and they see his shame. And **he gathered them together into a place called in the Hebrew tongue Armageddon**."* — Rev 16:12-16

The great river Euphrates is at the heart of the Assyrian and Babylonian empires. Obviously, this entire area is currently Muslim. The Euphrates River is already drying up so the kings of the east can cross to invade Israel and execute the "final solution" to destroy the Jew. I believe the term "kings of the east" refers to the Islamic nations once part of the Soviet Union, Afghanistan, Azerbaijan, Kazakhstan, Kyrgyz Republic, Pakistan, Tajikistan, Turkmenistan and Uzbekistan. All of these countries are presently aligned with Turkey and Iran in the Economic Cooperation Organization, the ECO. But that phrase could include China and India as well.

Three evil spirits like frogs are released from Satan, the Antichrist, and the False Prophet that work mighty deceiving miracles persuading the kings of the east to gather their armies, cross the Euphrates River and join in the battle at the valley of Megiddo, the battle of Armageddon. "Behold, I come as a thief..." with all the judgments and the time periods stated, how can the Lord come as a thief? Jesus states this in the Olivet discourse to his disciples in Matthew 24:36-44.

*'But of that day and hour knoweth no man, no, not the angels of heaven, but my Father only. But as the **days of Noe were, so shall also the coming of the Son of man be.** For as in the days that were before the flood they were eating and drinking, marrying and giving in marriage, until the day that Noe entered into the ark, **And knew not until the flood came, and took them all away; so shall also the coming of the Son of man be.** Then shall two be in the field; the **one shall be taken**, and the other left. Two women shall be grinding at the mill; the **one shall be taken**, and the other left. Watch therefore: for ye know not what hour your Lord doth come. But know this, that if the goodman of the house had known in what watch the thief would come, he would have watched, and would not have suffered his house to be broken up. Therefore be ye also ready: for **in such an hour as ye think not the Son of man cometh.**"*

The unbelievers of Noah's day did not know what was coming until the flood came and took them away. The flood took all unbelievers away. At the second coming of Jesus all unbelievers will be removed. The ones "taken away" are unbelievers removed from the earth at the second coming of Christ fulfilling the parable of the wheat and tares. Luke states in chapter 21:36

*"**Watch ye therefore**, and pray always, that ye may be accounted **worthy to escape** all these things that shall come to pass, and to **stand** before the Son of man."*

The Seventh Vial Judgment: Earthquake

*"And the **seventh angel** poured out his vial into the air; and there came a great voice out of the temple of heaven, from the throne,*

216

*saying, **It is done**. And there **were voices, and thunders, and lightnings; and there was a great earthquake**, such as was not since men were upon the earth, so mighty an earthquake, and so great. And the great city was divided into three parts, and the cities of the nation's fell: and great Babylon came in remembrance before God, to give unto her the cup of the wine of the fierceness of his wrath. And every island fled away, and the mountains were not found. And there **fell upon men a great hail out of heaven**, every stone about the weight of a talent: and men blasphemed God because of the plague of the hail; for the plague thereof was exceeding great." — Rev 16:17-21*

"It is done." The kingdoms in rebellion against the Most High God are fallen. The wrath of the winepress of God has been poured out and the mountains (kingdoms) were not found, and the islands (small independent nations) fled away.

Compare the seventh trumpet and the seventh vial. They are happening simultaneously with the voices, thunders, lightening, earthquakes and great hailstones the weight of a talent (70-100 lbs.).

217

Chapter Twenty Six
Mystery Babylon

*"And there came one of the seven angels which had the seven vials, and talked with me, saying unto me, Come hither; I will shew unto thee the judgment of the **great whore that sitteth upon many waters:** With whom the kings of the earth have committed fornication, and the inhabitants of the earth have been made **drunk with the wine of her fornication**. So he carried me away in the spirit **into the wilderness:** and I saw a **woman sit upon a scarlet coloured beast**, full of names of blasphemy, **having seven heads and ten horns**. And the woman was arrayed in purple and scarlet colour, and decked with gold and precious stones and pearls, having a golden cup in her hand full of abominations and filthiness of her fornication: And upon her forehead was a name written, **MYSTERY, BABYLON THE GREAT, THE MOTHER OF HARLOTS AND ABOMINATIONS OF THE EARTH.**" — Rev 17:1-5*

Chapters 17 and 18 happen in conjunction with the entire 7-year tribulation. The "Great Whore" that sits on many waters is an idolatrous religious system that sits on many peoples. The rulers of nations have partaken in her idolatry. Many places in the Old Testament the Lord labels idolatry as spiritual fornication. The Harlot has made many drunk with her wine of fornication (idolatry) which involves the shedding of blood in conquest of those that she has made drunk.

Notice that John is carried into the wilderness (desert) not the Italian peninsula. Last I checked, Rome was not in the middle of a desert. The harlot dwells in the desert and rides upon a scarlet-colored beast with seven heads and ten horns.

This beast is the ten horned (10 kingdom) empire of the Antichrist that we have seen in several texts. The fact that the beast is of a scarlet color implies that Satan has given his power to the beast. This is the ten-nation kingdom comprised of Middle Eastern Islamic nations. I will describe the seven heads shortly.

The harlot has the name **"MYSTERY, BABYLON THE GREAT, THE MOTHER OF HARLOTS AND ABOMINATIONS OF THE EARTH".** Babylon is a code word that means the seat or center of anti-Jehovah, anti-Christ, anti-Bible idolatry. It all started in ancient Babel which became Babylon. But in the New Testament we see that the Lord stated that Pergamum was the new seat of Satan. Later "Babylon" moved to Rome and then to Mecca. The center of anti-God, anti-Christ, anti-Israel, anti-Bible idolatry has been in Mecca for centuries.

Many students of prophecy believe that the Roman Catholic Church is the woman that rides the beast. Dave Hunt has a lengthy video and book on the subject. However, the Roman Catholic Church does not qualify for having a spirit of Antichrist because they do not deny the Son of God and they believe that He came in the flesh. The woman is not the Roman Catholic Church. Rome has no influence over any Middle Eastern nations, but Islam does. Islam rules them all, except Israel. If you know anything about Islam, you know they will never be part of another religion. Their goal is to bring the world to Islam. **The harlot is Mecca and Islam. The "MYSTERY" is that Mecca is the end times Babylon.**

If the context is actually physical Babylon, then what is the mystery? Ancient Babylon lies in ruin; if this is to be the seat of the Antichrist then much work needs to be done. Saddam Hussein tried to rebuild ancient Babylon but did not get far. It is basically an archeological site at present.

As we have seen in previous chapters, Islam is the spirit of Antichrist because the Koran specifically denies the Son of

God. Allah has no son. Whoever denies the Son has not the Father.

"And I saw the **woman drunken with the blood of the saints**, *and with the* **blood of the martyrs of Jesus**: *and when I saw her, I wondered with great admiration. And the angel said unto me, Wherefore didst thou marvel? I will tell thee the* **mystery of the woman**, *and of the beast that carrieth her, which hath the seven heads and ten horns.* **The beast that thou sawest was, and is not; and shall ascend out of the bottomless pit, and go into perdition**: *and they that dwell on the earth shall wonder, whose names were not written in the book of life from the foundation of the world, when they behold the beast that was, and is not, and yet is." — Rev 17:6-8*

The woman (Islam) is drunk with the blood of the saints and the martyrs of Jesus. I will get to the beast in a few verses.

"And **here is the mind which hath wisdom.** *The* **seven heads are seven mountains,** *on which the woman sitteth.* **And there are seven kings: five are fallen, and one is, and the other is not yet come; and when he cometh, he must continue a short space.** *And the* **beast that was, and is not, even he is the eighth, and is of the seven, and goeth into perdition.** *And the ten horns which thou sawest are* **ten kings,** *which have received no kingdom as yet; but receive power as kings one hour with the beast. These have one mind, and shall give their power and strength unto the beast. These shall make war with the Lamb, and the Lamb shall overcome them: for he is Lord of lords, and King of kings: and they that are with him are called, and chosen, and faithful. And he saith unto me,* **The waters** *which thou sawest, where the whore sitteth,* **are peoples, and multitudes, and nations, and tongues.** *And the ten horns which thou sawest upon the beast, these shall hate the whore, and shall make her desolate and naked, and shall eat her flesh, and burn her with fire. For God hath put in their*

hearts to fulfil his will, and to agree, and give their kingdom unto the beast, until the words of God shall be fulfilled. **And the woman which thou sawest is that great city, which reigneth over the kings of the earth.**" — *Rev 17:9-18*

- o The Seven Heads are seven mountains (kingdoms), seven kings.
- o Five are fallen, one is, and one is to come.
- o Beast 8 – Little Horn – takes over the 10 horned kingdom and reigns for 42 months.
- o The ten kings give their power to the beast to make war with the Lamb (Jesus).
- o The harlot controls many peoples.
- o The ten kings hate the harlot and destroy her with fire (Saddam sent scuds into Arabia towards Mecca) fulfilling the will of God. The Antichrist knows that the true Holy Place is in the Temple at Jerusalem, not Mecca.
- o The woman is a great city (center of spiritual fornication) – Mecca.

The traditional interpretation of the seven mountains is the kingdoms of Egypt, Assyria, Babylon, Media-Persia, Greece, Rome and revived Rome. However, as we have seen in the study of Daniel chapters two and seven, Rome is not in the hierarchy of Kingdoms ruling the Middle East. Then what might be the order of the seven kingdoms? Remember, each of the kingdoms must conquer Babylon; we are discussing Mystery Babylon right, not Mystery Jerusalem. We are in the times of the Gentiles.

We know from the study in Daniel that Babylon, Media-Persia, Greece, Islam/Ottoman, and a revived Islamic Empire rule the Middle East. If we add Egypt and Assyria to the list, then we have the seven kingdoms or heads. The text states that "one is" referring to the sixth kingdom. Many believe this references Rome because Rome was in power during the Apostle John's life. Why would the Holy Spirit place Rome in the hierarchy of kingdoms here in Revelation but not in the Book of

Daniel? The text clearly pictures John having a conversation with an angel, not in the 1st century A.D. but in the time frame of the last days. John and the angel are looking at the harlot, Mystery Babylon, riding the beast empire with 10 horns (kings) during the 7-year Tribulation.

The sixth kingdom that "is" pertains to the time of the last days not the 1st century. The religion of Islam is riding the beast; therefore, the Islamic Empire is the sixth kingdom of Revelation 17 and the fourth kingdom of Daniel chapters 2 and 7 just as previously stated.

The seventh kingdom is yet to come and continues only a brief time. This is the 10 horned kingdom from which the Antichrist arises and rules for the last 42 months of the seven-year tribulation. Here is the order of the first six kingdoms: Egypt, Assyria, Babylon, Media-Persia, Greece, and Islam/Ottoman empires. The seventh is a healed Ottoman Empire and continues only a short time leading into the eight which reigns for 3 ½ years controlled by the Antichrist.

"And after these things I saw another angel come down from heaven, having great power; and the earth was lightened with his glory. And he cried mightily with a strong voice, saying, **Babylon the great is fallen, is fallen, and is become the habitation of devils,** *and the hold of every foul spirit, and a cage of every unclean and hateful bird.* **For all nations have drunk of the wine of the wrath of her fornication, and the kings of the earth have committed fornication with her,** *and the merchants of the earth are waxed rich through the abundance of her delicacies. And I heard another voice from heaven, saying,* **Come out of her, my people,** *that ye be not partakers of her sins, and that ye receive not of her plagues. For her sins have reached unto heaven, and God hath remembered her iniquities. Reward her even as she rewarded you, and double unto her double according to her works: in the cup which she hath filled fill to her double. How much* **she hath glorified herself,** *and lived deliciously, so much torment and*

223

sorrow give her: for she saith in her heart, **I sit a queen, and am no widow,** *and shall see no sorrow. Therefore* **shall her plagues come in one day,** *death, and mourning, and famine; and she shall be utterly* **burned with fire:** *for strong is the Lord God who judgeth her."* — *Rev 18:1-8*

Babylon (idolatrous Babylon) is fallen, is fallen. This is the destruction of Mecca. The ancient city of Babylon is desolate, nothing more than an archeological site; she is not having spiritual fornication with anyone.

Mecca is committing spiritual fornication with every country in the Middle East save Israel. Many other countries are capitulating to the demands of Muslims, including America. Mecca has glorified herself as the spiritual center of Islam, the resting place of the image of Allah, the black stone in the Kaaba. Mecca sits as a queen over the realm of Islam. Mecca will be destroyed in one day, burned with fire.

"The earth is moved at the noise of their (Edom-Arabia) fall, at the cry the noise thereof was heard in the **Red sea***."* — *Jeremiah 49:21*

Many Muslim scholars have written that the Mahdi (the Islamic Messiah) will rule from Jerusalem since Mecca will be destroyed.

"And the **kings of the earth, who have committed fornication and lived deliciously with her, shall bewail her, and lament for her, when they shall see the smoke of her burning,** *Standing afar off for the fear of her torment, saying, Alas, alas, that great city Babylon, that mighty city! for* **in one hour is thy judgment come.** *And the merchants of the earth shall weep and mourn over her; for no man buyeth their merchandise any more: The merchandise of gold, and silver, and precious stones, and of pearls, and fine linen, and purple, and silk, and scarlet, and all thyine wood, and all manner vessels of*

224

ivory, and all manner vessels of most precious wood, and of brass, and iron, and marble, And cinnamon, and odours, and ointments, and frankincense, and wine, and oil, and fine flour, and wheat, and beasts, and sheep, and horses, and chariots, and slaves, and souls of men. And the fruits that thy soul lusted after are departed from thee, and all things which were dainty and goodly are departed from thee, and thou shalt find them no more at all. The merchants of these things, which were made rich by her, shall stand afar off for the fear of her torment, weeping and wailing, And saying, Alas, alas, that great city, that was clothed in fine linen, and purple, and scarlet, and decked with gold, and precious stones, and pearls! **For in one hour so great riches is come to nought. And every shipmaster, and all the company in ships, and sailors, and as many as trade by sea, stood afar off, And cried when they saw the smoke of her burning, saying, What city is like unto this great city!"** — *Rev 18:9-18*

The kings of the earth lament the destruction of Mecca. The list of goods are items that Arabia imports including slaves. There are many young people, slaves to indentured servitude, in Arabia. In one hour, all this will be destroyed. Sailors in the Red Sea will see the smoke of her burning.

"For it is **the day of the LORD'S vengeance**, *and the year of recompences for the* **controversy of Zion**. *And the streams thereof shall be* **turned into pitch**, *and the dust thereof into brimstone, and the* **land thereof shall become burning pitch**. *It shall not be quenched night nor day;* **the smoke thereof shall go up forever:** *from generation to generation it shall lie waste; none shall pass through it for ever and ever."* — *Isaiah 34:8-10 (the land of Idumea – Edom, Arabia)*

"And they **cast dust on their heads**, *and cried,* **weeping and wailing**, *saying, Alas, alas, that great city, wherein were made rich all that had ships in the sea by reason of her costliness! for in* **one hour is she**

225

*made desolate. Rejoice over her, thou heaven, and ye holy apostles and prophets; for God hath avenged you on her. And a mighty angel took up a stone like a great millstone, and cast it into the sea, saying, Thus with violence shall that great city Babylon be thrown down, and shall be found no more at all. And the voice of harpers, and musicians, and of pipers, and trumpeters, shall be heard no more at all in thee; and no craftsman, of whatsoever craft he be, shall be found any more in thee; and the sound of a millstone shall be heard no more at all in thee; And the light of a candle shall shine no more at all in thee; and the voice of the bridegroom and of the bride shall be heard no more at all in thee: for thy merchants were the great men of the earth; for **by thy sorceries were all nations deceived**. And in her was found the blood of prophets, and of saints, and of all that were slain upon the earth." — Rev 18:19-24*

Many will weep and wail over the destruction of spiritual Babylon. Many nations in the Middle East are deceived by the sorceries of Mecca and Islam. Muslims are known to cast dirt and dust on their heads as a sign of great grief.

Chäptër Twënty Sëvën
Thë Sëcänd Cäming

"And after these things I heard a great voice of much people in heaven, saying, **Alleluia; Salvation, and glory, and honour, and power, unto the Lord our God:** For true and righteous are his judgments: for he **hath judged the great whore,** which did corrupt the earth with her fornication, and hath avenged the blood of his servants at her hand. And again they said, Alleluia. **And her smoke rose up for ever and ever.** And the **four and twenty elders** and the four beasts fell down and worshipped God that sat on the throne, saying, Amen; Alleluia. And a voice came out of the throne, saying, Praise our God, all ye his servants, and ye that fear him, both small and great. And I heard as it were **the voice of a great multitude**, and as the voice of many waters, and as the voice of mighty thunderings, saying, Alleluia: for the Lord God omnipotent reigneth. Let us be glad and rejoice, and give honour to him: **for the marriage of the Lamb is come, and his wife hath made herself ready.** And to her was granted that she should be arrayed in fine linen, clean and white: for the fine linen is the righteousness of saints. And he saith unto me, Write, **Blessed are they which are called unto the marriage supper of the Lamb.** And he saith unto me, These are the true sayings of God. And I fell at his feet to worship him. And he said unto me, See thou do it not: I am thy fellowservant, and of thy brethren that have the testimony of Jesus: worship God: for the testimony of Jesus is the spirit of prophecy." — Rev 19:1–10

This is a fantastic scene in heaven around the Throne of God. Many are praising God for His true and righteous judgment of the great whore, Babylon (Mecca) whose burning smoke ascends forever.

*"And the streams thereof shall be **turned into pitch**, and the dust thereof into brimstone, and **the land thereof shall become burning pitch** It shall not be quenched night nor day; **the smoke thereof shall go up forever:** from generation to generation it shall lie waste; none shall pass through it for ever and ever."* — *Isaiah 34:9-10*

The voice of the heavenly multitude praising the Lord for the marriage is come. Jesus is about to return to earth and remarry Israel.

*"And I saw heaven opened, and **behold a white horse; and he that sat upon him was called Faithful and True, and in righteousness he doth judge and make war.** His eyes were as a **flame of fire**, and on his head were many crowns; and he had a name written, that no man knew, but he himself. And he was clothed with **a vesture dipped in blood:** and **his name is called The Word of God. And the armies which were in heaven followed him upon white horses, clothed in fine linen, white and clean.** And out of his mouth goeth a sharp sword, that with it **he should smite the nations:** and he shall **rule them with a rod of iron: and he treadeth the winepress of the fierceness and wrath of Almighty God.** And he hath on his vesture and on his thigh a name written, **KING OF KINGS, AND LORD OF LORDS.**"* — *Rev 19:11-16*

Wow, what a picture. I am afraid our finite minds can only get a mere glimpse of the magnitude of the real event; the Second Coming of the Lord Jesus Christ. He came the first time to shed His own blood for the sin of the world. At His Second

Coming He will shed the blood of the enemies of God and Israel for He comes in righteousness to "judge and make war". His eyes are a flame of fire and His robe dipped in blood. He is Jesus, The Word of God.

*"**Gird thy sword upon thy thigh**, O most mighty, with thy glory and thy majesty. And **in thy majesty ride prosperously** because of truth and meekness and righteousness; and thy right hand shall teach thee terrible things. Thine arrows are sharp in the heart of the king's enemies; whereby the people fall under thee. **Thy throne, O God, is for ever and ever: the sceptre of thy kingdom is a right sceptre.**"* — *Psalm 45:3-7*

The armies in heaven that follow Jesus are His Holy Angels, not church saints as many believe. Jesus will smite the nations and rule them with a rod of iron.

At His coming He will tread the winepress of the wrath of God that is being poured out upon the earth.

Isaiah 63:1-4 is simply amazing:

*"Who is this that cometh from **Edom**, with dyed garments from **Bozrah**? this that is glorious in his apparel, travelling in the greatness of his strength? I that speak in righteousness, mighty to save. **Wherefore art thou red in thine apparel**, and thy garments like him that treadeth in the winefat? **I have trodden the winepress alone**; and of the people there was none with me: for I will **tread them in mine anger**, and **trample them in my fury**; and **their blood shall be sprinkled upon my garments, and I will stain all my raiment. For the day of vengeance is in mine heart, and the year of my redeemed is come.**"*

*"His eyes shall see his destruction, and **he shall drink of the wrath of the Almighty.**"* — *Job 21:20*

229

*"Upon the wicked he shall rain snares, fire and brimstone, and an horrible tempest: **this shall be the portion of their cup.**"* — *Psalm 11:16*

*"**For in the hand of the LORD there is a cup**, and the wine is red; it is full of mixture; and he poureth out of the same: but the dregs thereof, **all the wicked of the earth shall wring them out, and drink them.**"* — *Psalm 75:8*

*"Awake, awake, stand up, **O Jerusalem**, which hast drunk at the hand of the LORD the cup of his fury; thou hast drunken the dregs of the cup of trembling, and wrung them out."* — *Isaiah 51:17*

*"Thus saith thy Lord the LORD, and thy God that pleadeth the cause of his people, **Behold, I have taken out of thine hand the cup of trembling, even the dregs of the cup of my fury; thou shalt no more drink it again:**"* — *Isaiah 51:22*

*"But with righteousness shall he judge the poor, and reprove with equity for the meek of the earth: and **he shall smite the earth with the rod of his mouth, and with the breath of his lips shall he slay the wicked.**"* — *Isaiah 11:4*

*"For thus saith the LORD God of Israel unto me; **Take the wine cup of this fury at my hand, and cause all the nations, to whom I send thee, to drink it.**"* — *Jeremiah 25:15*

Who shall drink from the cup of the wrath of God? The Book of Revelation does not list the countries involved in this judgment, but Jeremiah chapter 25 does.

*"And they shall drink, and be moved, and be mad, because of the sword that I will send among them. Then took I the cup at the LORD'S hand, and made all the nations to drink, unto whom the LORD had sent me: To wit, **Jerusalem**, and the **cities of Judah**, and the kings thereof, and the princes thereof, to make them a desolation, an astonishment, an hissing, and a curse; as it is this day; Pharaoh king of **Egypt**, and his servants, and his princes, and all his people; And all the mingled people, and all the kings of the land of **Uz**, and all the kings of the land of the **Philistines**, and Ashkelon, and Azzah, and Ekron, and the remnant of Ashdod, **Edom, and Moab, and the children of Ammon**, And all the kings of **Tyrus**, and all the kings of **Zidon**, and the kings of the isles which are beyond the sea, **Dedan, and Tema, and Buz**, and all that are in the utmost corners, And all the kings of **Arabia**, and all the kings of the **mingled people that dwell in the desert**, And all the kings of **Zimri**, and all the kings of **Elam**, and all the kings of the **Medes**, And all the kings of the north, far and near, one with another, and all the kingdoms of the world, which are upon the face of the earth: and the king of **Sheshach** shall drink after them."* — Jeremiah 25:16-26*

*"Thou shalt break them with a **rod of iron**; thou shalt dash them in pieces like a potter's vessel."* — Psalm 2:9*

Jerusalem, Judah, Egypt, Gaza, Jordan (Edom, Moab and Ammon), Lebanon (Tryus and Zidon), Arabia (Dedan, Tema, Buz and Zimri), Iran (Elam and Medes), Iraq (Sheshach). They are all Muslim nations that surround Israel. They will drink the cup of the Lord's wrath.

*"And I saw an angel standing in the sun; and he cried with a loud voice, saying to all the fowls that fly in the midst of heaven, **Come and gather yourselves together unto the supper of the great God;** That ye may eat the flesh of kings, and the flesh of captains, and the*

231

flesh of mighty men, and the flesh of horses, and of them that sit on them, and the flesh of all men, both free and bond, both small and great. **And I saw the beast, and the kings of the earth, and their armies, gathered together to make war against him that sat on the horse, and against his army.** *And the beast was taken, and with him the False Prophet that wrought miracles before him, with which he deceived them that had received the mark of the beast, and them that worshipped his image.* **These both were cast alive into a lake of fire burning with brimstone.** *And the* **remnant were slain with the sword of him that sat upon the horse,** *which sword proceeded out of his mouth: and all the fowls were filled with their flesh."* — *Rev 19:17-21*

A call goes out to the fowls of heaven, come to God's supper. The beast kingdom and the Antichrist are gathered to make war against the returning Lord Jesus and His angelic army. The Antichrist and the False Prophet are cast alive into the lake of fire and their followers slain by the Lord. The supper of the great God is served. The flesh of the wicked is on the menu.

"And, thou son of man, thus saith the Lord GOD; Speak unto every feathered fowl, and to every beast of the field, Assemble yourselves, and come; **gather yourselves on every side to my sacrifice that I do sacrifice for you, even a great sacrifice upon the mountains of Israel, that ye may eat flesh, and drink blood.** *Ye shall eat the flesh of the mighty, and drink the blood of the princes of the earth, of rams, of lambs, and of goats, of bullocks, all of them* **fatlings of Bashan.** *And ye shall eat fat till ye be full, and drink blood till ye be drunken, of my sacrifice which I have sacrificed for you."* — *Ezekiel 39:17-19*

Revelation chapter 20 opens with Satan being bound for a thousand years.

*"And I saw an angel come down from heaven, having the key of the bottomless pit and a great chain in his hand. And **he laid hold on the dragon, that old serpent, which is the Devil, and Satan, and bound him a thousand years**, And cast him into the bottomless pit, and shut him up, and set a seal upon him, that he should deceive the nations no more, till the thousand years should be fulfilled: and after that **he must be loosed a little season.**" — Rev 20:1-3*

Satan is caught and cast into the pit and held with a great chain. During the thousand-year reign of Christ, Satan is bound and cannot deceive the nations.

*"In that day the LORD with his sore and great and strong sword shall **punish leviathan the piercing serpent**, even leviathan that crooked serpent; and he shall **slay the dragon** that is in the sea."* — *Isaiah 27:1*

However, after the thousand years is fulfilled, Satan is loosed for a little season. Why is he let loose? He is let loose to tempt those that have been born during the millennial reign of the Lord Jesus Christ. Those people have lived in a near perfect world and have not been tempted by the devil so they must endure a short period of temptation; their sin nature must be tested.

*"And I saw thrones, and they sat upon them, and judgment was given unto them: and I saw the souls of them that were **beheaded for the witness of Jesus**, and for the word of God, and which had **not worshipped the beast, neither his image, neither had received his mark upon their foreheads, or in their hands; and they lived and reigned with Christ a thousand years**. But the rest of the dead lived not again until the thousand years were finished. **This is the first resurrection**. Blessed and holy is he that hath part in the first*

*resurrection: on such the **second death hath no power,** but they shall be priests of God and of Christ, and **shall reign with him a thousand years.**" — Rev 20:4-6*

The souls of the tribulation saints, those beheaded for their witness of Jesus, are before the throne in heaven. These are obviously tribulation saints because they did not take the mark of the beast nor worship him. This characteristic places them within the 7-year tribulation. These saints are raised from the dead and given their glorified bodies. This event completes the "first resurrection". This is part of the resurrection of the just over which the second death (lake of fire) has no power. These resurrected tribulation saints will rule and reign with Christ, during the thousand-year kingdom.

*"And **when the thousand years are expired, Satan shall be loosed** out of his prison, And shall go out **to deceive the nations** which are in the four quarters of the earth, **Gog and Magog, to gather them together to battle:** the number of whom is as the sand of the sea. And they went up on the breadth of the earth, and compassed the camp of the saints about, and the beloved city: and **fire came down from God out of heaven, and devoured them.** And the devil that deceived them was cast into the lake of fire and brimstone, where the beast and the False Prophet are, and shall be tormented day and night for ever and ever." — Rev 20:7-10*

After the thousand-year reign of the Lord Jesus Christ, Satan is released to deceive the nations. He will muster an army of those not willing to be ruled by Jesus. This rebellion will happen in the area of Asia Minor just as before. The army is destroyed by fire from God. The devil is cast into the lake of fire to join the Antichrist, the False Prophet. There they will be tormented forever.

*"And I saw a **great white throne**, and him that sat on it, from whose face the earth and the heaven fled away; and there was found no place for them. And **I saw the dead, small and great, stand before God**; and the books were opened: and another book was opened, which is the book of life: and the **dead were judged** out of those things which were written in the books, **according to their works**. And the sea gave up the dead which were in it; and death and hell delivered up the dead which were in them: and they were judged every man **according to their works**. And death and hell were cast into the lake of fire. **This is the second death. And whosoever was not found written in the book of life was cast into the lake of fire.**" — Rev 20:11-15*

The great white throne judgment is a judgment of the unbelieving dead from the beginning of mankind. They are resurrected and judged according to their works. That will determine the level of punishment they will receive in the lake of fire. This is the second death; a second physical and spiritual death separated from God in the lake of fire.

*"And I saw a **new heaven and a new earth**: for the first heaven and the first earth were passed away; and there was no more sea. And I John saw the holy city, **new Jerusalem**, coming down from God out of heaven, prepared as a bride adorned for her husband. And I heard a great voice out of heaven saying, Behold, **the tabernacle of God is with men**, and he will dwell with them, and they shall be his people, and God himself shall be with them, and be their God. And God shall **wipe away all tears from their eyes**; and there shall be **no more death**, neither sorrow, nor crying, **neither shall there be any more pain**: for the former things are passed away. And he that sat upon the throne said, Behold, **I make all things new**. And he said unto me, Write: for these words are true and faithful. And he said unto me, It is done. I am Alpha and Omega, the beginning and the end. I will*

give unto him that is athirst of the fountain of the water of life freely. **He that overcometh shall inherit all things***; and I will be his God, and he shall be my son.   But the fearful, and unbelieving, and the abominable, and murderers, and whoremongers, and sorcerers, and idolaters, and all liars, shall have their part in the lake which burneth with fire and brimstone: which is the* **second death***.” — Rev 20:1-8*

After the great white throne judgment and all evil is cast into the lake of fire, a new heaven and a new earth appear. Then the New Jerusalem descends from heaven and the tabernacle of God is with men. In this new era everything is brand new. No more tears, no more death, no more sorrow, no more crying, no more pain, all these are passed away. All this is for the saints. All others are partakers in the second death.

“And there came unto me one of the seven angels which had the seven vials full of the seven last plagues, and talked with me, saying, Come hither, **I will shew thee the bride, the Lamb's wife***.   And he carried me away in the spirit to a great and high mountain,* **and shewed me that great city, the holy Jerusalem, descending out of heaven from God, Having the glory of God***: and her light was like unto a stone most precious, even like a jasper stone, clear as crystal; And had a wall great and high, and had* **twelve gates***, and at the gates twelve angels, and names written thereon, which are the names of the* **twelve tribes of the children of Israel***:   On the east three gates; on the north three gates; on the south three gates; and on the west three gates.   And the wall of the city had* **twelve foundations***, and in them the names of the* **twelve apostles of the Lamb***.   And he that talked with me had a golden reed to measure the city, and the gates thereof, and the wall thereof.   And the city lieth foursquare, and the length is as large as the breadth: and he measured the city with the reed,* **twelve thousand furlongs***.   The length and the breadth and the height of it are equal.   And he measured the wall thereof, an hundred and forty and four*

cubits, according to the measure of a man, that is, of the angel. And the building of the wall of it was of jasper: and the city was pure gold, like unto clear glass. And the foundations of the wall of the city were garnished with all manner of precious stones. The first foundation was jasper; the second, sapphire; the third, a chalcedony; the fourth, an emerald; The fifth, sardonyx; the sixth, sardius; the seventh, chrysolite; the eighth, beryl; the ninth, a topaz; the tenth, a chrysoprasus; the eleventh, a jacinth; the twelfth, an amethyst. And the twelve gates were twelve pearls; every several gate was of one pearl: and the street of the city was pure gold, as it were transparent glass." — Rev 21:9-21

The New Jerusalem is the permanent home of all that are in Christ from Adam to the end of the Millennial Reign. The dimensions are 1500 miles on each side. This area is half the size of the continental USA.

*"And I saw **no temple therein**: for the **Lord God Almighty and the Lamb are the temple of it**. And the city had **no need of the sun, neither of the moon**, to shine in it: for **the glory of God did lighten it, and the Lamb is the light thereof**. And the nations of them which are saved shall walk in the light of it: and the kings of the earth do bring their glory and honour into it. And the gates of it shall not be shut at all by day: for there **shall be no night there**. And they shall bring the glory and honour of the nations into it. And there shall in no wise enter into it any thing that defileth, neither whatsoever worketh abomination, or maketh a lie: **but they which are written in the Lamb's book of life**." — Rev 21:22-27*

The New Jerusalem will shine with the glory and light of the Father and the Son. There is no need for a sun or a moon for God is the light. The city will be occupied by those whose names are written in the Lamb's book of life.

"And he shewed me a pure river of water of life, clear as crystal, proceeding out of the throne of God and of the Lamb. In the midst of the street of it, and on either side of the river, was there the tree of life, which bare twelve manner of fruits, and yielded her fruit every month: and the leaves of the tree were for the healing of the nations. And there shall be **no more curse***: but the throne of God and of the Lamb shall be in it; and his servants shall serve him: And they shall see his face; and his name shall be in their foreheads. And there shall be no night there; and they need no candle, neither light of the sun; for the Lord God giveth them light: and* **they shall reign for ever and ever.***" — Rev 22:1-5*

In the New Jerusalem there will be a pure river of the water of life for all to drink and the tree of life for all to eat. There is no more curse as was on the old earth, the curse of sin. We shall see the face of God and reign with Him for ever and ever. The pure river of the water of life is the pure Word of God that will continually go forth unto the nations.

"And he said unto me, **These sayings are faithful and true***: and the Lord God of the holy prophets sent his angel to shew unto his servants the things which must shortly be done.* **Behold, I come quickly: blessed is he that keepeth the sayings of the prophecy of this book.** *And I John saw these things, and heard them. And when I had heard and seen, I fell down to worship before the feet of the angel which shewed me these things. Then saith he unto me, See thou do it not: for I am thy fellowservant, and of thy brethren the prophets, and of them which keep the sayings of this book: worship God. And he saith unto me,* **Seal not the sayings of the prophecy of this book: for the time is at hand.** *He that is unjust, let him be unjust still: and he which is filthy, let him be filthy still: and he that is righteous, let him be righteous still: and he that is holy, let him be holy still." — Rev 22:6-11*

The words of this prophecy are faithful and true. We are living in the last days of the dispensation of grace. Once the rapture removes the church, the body of Christ, from the earth, the 7-year Tribulation will begin culminating with the second coming of Jesus Christ.

*"And, **behold, I come quickly; and my reward is with me, to give every man according as his work shall be. I am Alpha and Omega,** the beginning and the end, the first and the last. **Blessed are they that do his commandments, that they may have right to the tree of life, and may enter in through the gates into the city.** For without are dogs, and sorcerers, and whoremongers, and murderers, and idolaters, and whosoever loveth and maketh a lie. I Jesus have sent mine angel to testify unto you these things in the churches. I am the root and the offspring of David, and the bright and morning star. And the Spirit and the bride say, Come. And let him that heareth say, Come. And let him that is athirst come. And whosoever will, let him take the water of life freely. For I testify unto every man that heareth the words of the prophecy of this book, **If any man shall add unto these things, God shall add unto him the plagues that are written in this book: And if any man shall take away from the words of the book of this prophecy, God shall take away his part out of the book of life,** and out of the holy city, and from the things which are written in this book. He which testifieth these things saith, **Surely I come quickly. Amen. Even so, come, Lord Jesus.** The grace of our Lord Jesus Christ be with you all. Amen." — Rev 22:12-21*

What a salutation to a magnificent book that mere words cannot do justice. The Lord says, "behold, I come quickly". Blessed are those that walk in obedience for they have a right to eat from the tree of life and enter into the gates of the New Jerusalem.

239

A stern warning to those that would profane the words of this prophecy. If anyone adds to these words, God will add to him the plagues of His wrath defined herein. If anyone would take away from this prophecy, God will remove his name from the Lamb's book of life.

Surely, I come quickly. Amen.
Even so, Come, Lord Jesus.

Part Eleven

Islam Satan's Masterpiece

Chapter Twenty Eight

The Real Muhammad

To properly understand groups like Hamas, Hezbollah, Islamic Jihad, the PLO, the PA, the Muslim Brotherhood, and others, one must look to their prophet Muhammad. We have all seen the flags, banners, and headbands of ISIS, Hamas, and Hezbollah, but what do these flags represent?

The stylized writing on their flags is the shahada which is the statement "there is no god but Allah and Muhammad is his messenger." This is the profession of faith for Muslims.

The seal on some flags is the Seal of Muhammad. This is the seal they believe Muhammad used to authenticate documents and letters when he was alive. The seal proclaims that the members are strict followers of Muhammad and emulate his actions and lifestyle. This is why it is critical that we understand the real Muhammad.
The Early Years in Mecca:

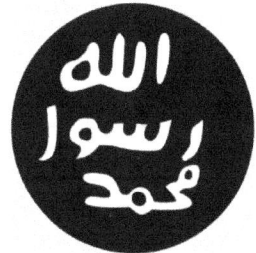

241

Mohammad was born around A. D. 570 in Mecca, Saudi Arabia. His father died before he was born, and his mother died when he was six year old. He was raised by his uncle and as a young man worked as a camel driver for a trading company owned by a woman named Khadija. He made many excursions to the Levant with the caravans. When he was twenty five, he married Khadija.

Discontent with the 360 pagan gods of Mecca, Mohammad would retreat to the nearby Mount Hira for rest and meditation. In A. D. 610 on one of his retreats to Mount Hira he claimed to have a visitation from the angel Gabriel. During this and subsequent visitations he was given a body of revelation that would soon become the Quran, the holy book of Islam. The Quran is said to be revelation from Allah.

Mohammad thought he was mad after the first visitation from the angel, but Khadija proclaimed him to be a prophet of God. Mohammad soon accepted this title and proclaimed himself a prophet in the lineage of Abraham and Jesus. He promised to consolidate the pagan gods of Mecca into one god, Allah, the moon god. After several years of street preaching, he gathered about one hundred followers.

He began to ridicule and mock the Meccans for not following him and becoming a Muslim. Mecca was an open society and they resented Mohammad's mockery of their beliefs and lifestyle. He also cursed the religion of the Jews and Christians because they rejected him as a Biblical prophet. They knew from his early days of street preaching that he was a False Prophet.

A quote from a Muslim scholar states: "The Meccans said they had never known anything like the trouble they had endured from this fellow. He had declared their mode of life foolish, insulted their forefathers, reviled their religion, divided the community, and cursed their gods" (Ibn Ishaq/Hisham 183). The Meccans made an offer of peace to Mohammad around A. D. 620, but he rejected it. Shortly thereafter he makes a treaty with the tribes of Medina to make war with Mecca. At this point

the Meccans had enough of Mohammad. They banish him from the city and he and family fled to Medina.
Medina, Mohammad's rise to power:

While in Medina Mohammad begins raiding the caravans from Mecca. However, he still has only a small group of followers. He receives a convenient revelation from Allah that if he would share the booty from the caravan raids with his followers then his army would grow. Grow it did, within a few years he had about ten thousand men that followed him. Well, the Meccans started sending out their army to protect their caravans. Mohammad's first battle was the battle of Badr in A. D. 624 where he defeated the Meccan army and captured the caravan. This was the beginning of Jihad, wars against unbelievers.

During this time of raiding caravans and raising an army, Mohammad's hatred for the Jews grew. He hated them for not believing he was a legitimate prophet. They rejected his homemade renditions of the Old Testament Bible stories. The Jews knowledge of the Word threatened Mohammad's credibility and the validity of Islam. The Jews of the Banu Qaynuqa tribe in Medina were the first to feel the hatred of Mohammad. With his growing army supporting him, he forced these Jews into exile and confiscated their homes, property, and belongings all under the guise that a Jew insulted a Muslim woman. Insulting Islam still carries the threat of death. This photo was taken in London showing some of the proponents of the religion of peace.

Emboldened by his success, Mohammad seized upon the Banu Nadir tribe in Medina. After killing many of the prominent Jews he accused them of plotting to kill him. Next, he

243

raided the Banu Qurayza Jewish tribe and executed every male over the age of twelve. Mohammad personally killed over 800 men that day. Old people were banished, young women were raped and taken as sex slaves, property and homes were confiscated all in the name of Allah and Islam. Muslim apologists will try to hide or deny this, but it is historical fact.

For the past 1300+ years Muslims have killed Christians and Jews (both infidels) thinking they are doing the will of Allah. Jesus said *"the time cometh, that whosoever killeth you will think that he doeth God service"* John 16:2. I was puzzled by that verse of Scripture until I started studying Islam. Now it makes perfect sense.

In A. D. 622 Khadija dies and Mohammad marries Aisha, age 9, that's right, nine. Over the next ten years he had 11 more wives, several at one time. In A. D. 628 Mohammad makes a ten-year treaty with the Meccans called the Treaty of Hudaibiya. The purpose of this treaty was to build up arms and lull the Meccans into a false sense of peace and safety. Two years later he attacks the Meccans by surprise and conquers the city. In A.D. 632 Mohammad dies, but not before conquering the entire Arabian Peninsula.

The following quote from www.bibleprobe.com sums up Mohammad's life. "As you can see, Muhammad posed as an apostle of God. Yet his life is filled with lustfulness (12 marriages and sex with a child, slaves and concubines), rapes, warfare, conquests, and unmerciful butcheries. What Muhammad produced in the Qur'an is simply a book of gibberish consisting of later evil verses abrogating (superseding) earlier peaceful verses. These verses in Arabic poetically "tickle" the ears of Arab listeners. Islam is a caustic blend of paganism and twisted Bible stories. Muhammad, its lone "prophet", who made no prophecies, conceived his religion to satiate his lust for power, sex, and money. He was a terrorist."

The modern Islamic groups that emulate Muhammad display the same barbaric actions and should be dealt with accordingly. Negotiations with them are a sign of weakness.

244

Sadly, the one thing they understand is force, overwhelming force.

Chäptër Twënty Ninë

Just whä is Alläh

Ancient Sumerians from Mesopotamia worshipped the moon god using the names Suen, Nana and Asimbabber. The Assyrians and Babylonians changed the name Suen to Sin. Sin was signified by the crescent phase of the moon. This image is a Cylinder-seal of Khashkhamer, patesi of Ishkun-Sin (in North Babylonia), and vassal of Ur-Engur, king of Ur (c. 2400 BC) (British Museum). The worship of the crescent moon god Sin is clearly depicted. Please note that this artifact is dated circa 2400 B.C., three thousand years before the birth of Muhammad.

The Stela of Nabonidus Neo-Babylonian dynasty, 555-539 BC (British Museum). The moon-god Sin (closest to him), the winged disc of the sun-god Shamash and the planet Venus of Ishtar celebrates the return of plenty after a drought. Nabonidus was the son of Nebuchadnezzar, king of Babylon who took the nation of Israel captive around the turn of the sixth century B. C.

The next image is that of Kudurru of Babylonian King Melishishu II, 1202-1188 B.C. (Louvre, Paris) who presents his daughter (holding a harp) to Nanai, goddess of health and medicine. The moon god Sin is clearly depicted by the crescent phase symbol. There are many similar artifacts in the British Museum, the Louvre, and other fine museums around the world. I have chosen just three to make the point that the worship of the moon god predates Islam by thousands of years. Allah, the god of Islam, is simply a makeover of the ancient Babylonian pagan moon god Sin. The reality is that Allah is no god; he is merely a fabrication of Satan whose plan is to deceive many thereby condemning their souls to hell. There truly is nothing new under the sun. In fact, if you entertain a detailed study of the god of Islam you will discover that Allah is not the God of the Bible but clearly the antithesis.

In the book of Judges Chapter 8 we read how the Lord raised up Gideon to fight the kings of Midian (Arabia). After defeating the armies of Midian, the two kings of Midian, Zebah and Zalmunna, flee from the battle. Gideon gives chase and catches them. We join the narrative in verse 21:

"So Zebah and Zalmunna said, "Rise yourself, and kill us; for as a man is, so is his strength." So Gideon arose and killed Zebah and Zalmunna, and took the crescent ornaments that were on their camels' necks." We read in verse 21 "Now the weight of the gold earrings that he requested was one thousand seven hundred shekels of gold, besides the crescent ornaments, pendants, and purple robes which were on the kings of Midian, and besides the chains that were around their camels' necks." The kings of Midian wore purple robes. The great whore, mystery Babylon is also dressed in purple.

248

Notice the crescent ornaments of gold that were about the necks of the kings and their camels. These were the ancient ornaments of the moon god Sin. Here we see from Scripture the ancient tribes of Arabia worshiped the false moon god Sin. The crescent moon ornament is still the symbol of the moon god and clearly seen atop Islamic mosques and minarets and on the flags of many Muslim nations.

Beware of men like George W. Bush, Rick Warren and the late Robert Schuller that proclaim Christians and Muslims worship the same god. Beware of churches that promote union with Muslims under the banner of "love your neighbor" or "Jesus in the Quran" teachings or Chrislam. These folks are heretics given over to doctrines of demons as stated by the Apostle Paul in his first epistle to Timothy *"Now the Spirit speaketh expressly, that in the latter times some shall depart from the faith, giving heed to seducing spirits, and doctrines of devils;"* - 1 Timothy 4:1 KJV.

The Apostle Paul gave us clear instruction in dealing with these people. "*And have no fellowship with the unfruitful works of darkness, but rather reprove them.*" Ephesians 5:11 KJV.

"This know also, that in the last days perilous times shall come. For men shall be lovers of their own selves, covetous, boasters, proud, blasphemers, disobedient to parents, unthankful, unholy, Without natural affection, trucebreakers, false accusers, incontinent, fierce, despisers of those that are good, Traitors, heady, highminded, lovers of pleasures more than lovers of God; Having a form of godliness, but denying the power thereof: from such turn away." - 2 Timothy 3:1–5 KJV

Yes, that's correct, expose them and have nothing to do with them.

Chapter Thirty

The Jesus of Islam

People have said to me in an apologetic or even defensive tone of voice "well, Jesus is in the Quran." Immediately I know that these either have an agenda contrary to the Bible or are willfully ignorant of the Jesus in the Quran. Let's take a look at what the Quran states about Jesus or Isa as he is named therein.

"How shall I bear a child,' she Mary answered, 'when I am a virgin...?' 'Such is the will of the Lord,' he replied. 'That is no difficult thing for Him...God forbid that He God Himself should beget a son!...Those who say: 'The Lord of Mercy has begotten a son,' preach a monstrous falsehood..." (Surah 19:12-, 29-, 88)

Even though Muslims believe in the virgin birth of Jesus they do not believe that Jesus is the Son of God. They believe that Jesus was just another prophet. Proclaiming that Jesus is the only begotten Son of God as the Bible clearly states is to "preach a monstrous falsehood." Some additional quotes from the Quran:

- o "They say: 'God has begotten a son.' God forbid! Self-sufficient is He." (Surah 10:68)
- o "Furthermore, this divine writ is meant to warn all those who assert, "God has taken unto Himself a son." (Surah 18:4)
- o "it is inconceivable that the Most Gracious should take unto Himself a son!" (Surah 19:92)

Allah is self-sufficient; he has no need of a son. It is inconceivable that Allah would take a son. Those that say such things are to be warned of their error. Such is the teaching of the

Quran about our precious Lord and Savior, Jesus Christ. More quotes:

- o "God has begotten a son"; and, verily, they are lying too, when they say," (Surah 37:152)
- o "Had God willed to take Unto Himself a son, He could have chosen anyone that He wanted out of whatever He has created - but limitless is He in His glory! He is the One God, the One who holds absolute sway over all that exists!" (Surah 39:3-4)

The Quran teaches that if you say that Allah has begotten a son you are a liar. Allah has no need for a son since he holds absolute power over all that exists. If Allah wanted a son he could have picked whomever he wanted. Clearly the Jesus of Islam is another Jesus. The Apostle Paul states:

"But though we, or an angel from heaven, preach any other gospel unto you than that which we have preached unto you, let him be accursed." - Galatians 1:8 KJV.

Still more quotes:
- o "for we know that sublimely exalted is our Sustainer's majesty: no consort has He ever taken unto Himself, nor a son!" (Surah 72:3)
- o "And yet some people assert, "God has taken unto Himself a son!" Limitless is He in His glory! Nay, but His is all that is in the heavens and on earth; all things devoutly obey His will." (Surah 2:96,116)
- o "He begets not, and neither is He begotten" (Surah 112:3)
- o "He to whom the dominion over the heavens and the earth belongs, and who begets no offspring, [2] and has no partner in His dominion: for it is He who creates every thing and determines its nature in accordance with His own design." (Surah 25:2)

251

It should be crystal clear by now that Allah has no son and has no need of a son; Allah begets not. Here are some quotes from the Bible to solidify the contrast between the Jesus of the Quran and the real Jesus of the Bible.

*"No man hath seen God at any time; the **only begotten Son**, which is in the bosom of the Father, he hath declared him." – John 1:18 KJV*

*"For God so loved the world, that he gave his **only begotten Son**, that whosoever believeth in him should not perish, but have everlasting life. ... He that believeth on him is not condemned: but he that believeth not is condemned already, because he hath not believed in the name of the **only begotten Son of God**." – John 3:16, 18 KJV*

*"In this was manifested the love of God toward us, because that God sent his **only begotten Son** into the world, that we might live through him." – 1 John 4:9 KJV*

Remember, Allah begets not.

*"I will declare the decree: the LORD hath said unto me, Thou art my Son; **this day have I begotten thee**." – Psalm 2:7 KJV*

*"God hath fulfilled the same unto us their children, in that he hath raised up Jesus again; as it is also written in the second psalm, **Thou art my Son, this day have I begotten thee**." – Acts 13:33 KJV*

*"For unto which of the angels said he at any time, Thou art my Son, this day have **I begotten thee**? And again, I will be to him a Father, and he shall be to me a Son?" – Hebrews 1:5 KJV*

*"So also Christ glorified not himself to be made an high priest; but he that said unto him, Thou art my Son, **today have I begotten thee.**" - Hebrews 5:5 KJV*

And of course:

*"And Jesus, when he was baptized, went up straightway out of the water: and, lo, the heavens were opened unto him, and he saw the Spirit of God descending like a dove, and lighting upon him: And lo a voice from heaven, saying, **This is my beloved Son, in whom I am well pleased.**" - Matthew 3:16-17 KJV*

The Jesus of the Bible and the Jesus of the Quran are mutually exclusive; they are completely antithetical. They are exact opposites having nothing in common. The spirit of Allah and the Quran are Antichrist as proclaimed by the Apostle John.

"Who is a liar but he that denieth that Jesus is the Christ? He is Antichrist, that denieth the Father and the Son." - 1 John 2:22 KJV

"And every spirit that confesseth not that Jesus Christ is come in the flesh is not of God: and this is that spirit of Antichrist, whereof ye have heard that it should come; and even now already is it in the world." - 1 John 4:3 KJV

"For many deceivers are entered into the world, who confess not that Jesus Christ is come in the flesh. This is a deceiver and an Antichrist." - 2 John 1:7 KJV

The Scriptures are clear and profound. The Quran, the Muslim Jesus and the teachings of Muhammad are totally contrary to the Bible. They are from the spirit of Antichrist, Satan himself. The God of Abraham, Isaac and Jacob is not the god of Islam.

There is another very interesting quote from that Quran that has profound implications.

"and their boast, "Behold, we have slain the Christ Jesus, son of Mary, who claimed to be an apostle of God!" However, they did not slay him, and neither did they crucify him, but it only seemed to them as if it had been so; and, verily, those who hold conflicting views thereon are indeed confused, having no real knowledge thereof, and following mere conjecture. For, of a certainty, they did not slay him:" (Surah 4:151,157)

According to the Quran, Jesus was not crucified. If Jesus was not crucified, then His blood was not shed for our sins. If that be the case, then we are still dead in our sins without any hope of eternal life with God. Also, Jesus is no Lord and certainly no Savior. This is another satanic lie from the pit of hell. The Islamic Jesus is a satanic counterfeit sent to deceive and condemn to hell those who follow Muhammad.

Chapter Thirty One
Islamic Worldview

The Quran clearly teaches Muslims on how to treat Christians, Jews, and unbelievers. Here are some teachings from the Quran:

- "Muhammad is God's apostle. Those who follow him are ruthless to the unbelievers but merciful to one another." (Surah 48:29)
- "Fight against such as those to whom the Scriptures were given Jews and Christians...until they pay tribute out of hand and are utterly subdued." (Surah 9:27)

Does the Bible teach Christians to be ruthless to unbelievers? Of course not, we are to love and pray for them. Muslims are taught to be merciful only to Muslims and ruthless to the unbeliever. They are to fight against Christians and Jews and to utterly subdue them; in other words, to conquer them. Does this teaching sound like God or Satan? Terms like ruthlessly fight and utterly subdue Christians and Jews can only be attributed to Satan.

- "If you fear treachery from any of your allies, you may fairly retaliate by breaking off your treaty with them." (Surah 8:51)
- "O YOU who have attained to faith! Do not take the Jews and the Christians for your allies:" (Surah 5:51)
- "Seek out your enemies relentlessly." (Surah 4:103)

Here Muslims are taught to lie and break treaties. They are not to take Christians and Jews for friends and allies. Pursue your enemies relentlessly. Sounds like more of the same and completely contrary to the teachings of the Bible.

- o "Fighting is obligatory for you, much as you dislike it." (Surah 2:216)
- o "The only true faith in God's sight is Islam." (Surah 3:19)
- o "Slay them wherever you find them...Idolatry is worse than carnage...Fight against them until idolatry is no more and God's religion reigns supreme." (Surah 2:190-)

Idolatry (the teachings of the Bible) is considered worse than bloodshed. Muslims are taught to fight until Islam reigns supreme over the world. The Muslim new world order is everything brought under subjection to Islam through fighting and wars.

"Indeed, the truth deny they who say, "Behold, God is the third of a trinity" - seeing that there is no deity whatever save the One God. And unless they desist from this their assertion, grievous suffering is bound to befall such of them as are bent on denying the truth." (Surah 5:73)

Here we read that the Quran denies the doctrine of the Trinity proclaimed by the Bible. One God in essence expressed to humanity in three persons (Father, Son and Holy Spirit). Again, the spirit of Islam is the spirit of Antichrist.

Conclusions:
1. Allah is a false pagan moon god.
2. Islam is the religion of the Antichrist spirit (Satan).
3. Muhammad is a false perverted prophet.
4. The Jesus of Islam is a false blasphemous Jesus.

5. The Quran is a fake holy book completely contrary to the Holy Bible.

It is quite easy to see that the Bible and the Quran are incompatible in their doctrines. But it does not stop there. We must understand that Islam is not simply another pagan religion.

Islam is a theocratic government that seeks to control every aspect of political, social, economic and personal life. This is why they seek to implement Sharia law everywhere they emigrate. Islam is entirely incompatible with Christianity and America.

Since Islam is a theocratic government contrary to our Constitution, no Constitutional rights or protections should be extended to Islam or its followers. It is a hostile foreign government seeking to supplant the Constitution of the United States, our form of government and the American way of life. It cannot be tolerated in a free society. Freedom does not extend to those seeking to overthrow our government and corrupt our society. Pray for America.

Thank You, I hope you have enjoyed our study in end times Bible prophecy.

Paul Felter

www.ingramcontent.com/pod-product-compliance
Lightning Source LLC
Chambersburg PA
CBHW071221290326
41931CB00037B/1585